MARY PIX

THE CONQUEST OF SPAIN

edited by David McDevitt

Los Angeles, California

Copyright © 2021

David McDevitt

Bluebook Publishing House

All rights reserved

ISBN: 978-0-578-99791-9

About the Author

Mary Pix was born Mary Griffith in 1666 in Oxfordshire, England. In 1684, she married George Pix, and they had one child who died young. Pix rose to prominence as a professional playwright relatively late in life with her first and most enduring play, *Ibrahim, the Thirteenth Emperor of the Turks* (1696). She avoided most of the time period's slanders aimed at professional women playwrights, and she wrote more than a dozen plays over the course of her career. *The Conquest of Spain* (1705) was initially performed without Pix's name attached to it, but her name appeared on the printed version that was published later that same year. *The Conquest of Spain* was the last tragedy and the second-to-last play of Pix's career before her death in 1709.

About the Editor

David McDevitt attended Arizona State University for his bachelor's degree in English literature and then California State University, Long Beach for his master's degree in English. He discovered Mary Pix during his graduate studies but was unable to find any convenient edition of *The Conquest of Spain*: a gap that this book aims to fill. David is a lecturer of English literature and composition in southern California where he lives with his wife and daughter.

Editor's Note

The copy text for this book is the 1705 edition available digitally or as a printed facsimile from Early English Books Online. Capitalization has been updated to modern standards, including using lower-case letters for abstract nouns used figuratively as personifications (e.g. "love," "death"). All words have been updated to modern spelling except when two or more meanings are possible, in which cases I have included footnotes to explain possible meanings. Punctuation has also been quietly updated, if not quite to modern perfection, then much closer to it and more in line with the apparent intended meanings and rhythms of the text.

Scene changes are new to this edition and have been added every time the stage is empty. Other non-speech text has also been quietly updated where doing so does not change the meaning of the text (e.g. replacing "Exit" with "Exeunt" or attributing speeches to "Don Gomez" instead of "Governor"). Line numbers are included for every five lines of speech. Given Pix's inconsistent meter, I have taken a uniform approach to line numbers; when one line of meter is spoken by two or more different speakers, I have treated each speaker's words as a new line.

Edited stage directions, speech attributions, settings, and any other words that change or add to the meaning of the original text have been placed in square brackets. Footnotes are included on every page and are meant as references only so are not indicated in the text of the play itself. Most footnotes offer a short definition, paraphrase, or clarification while others explain references, alternate meanings, and editorial choices.

My purpose in creating this volume is to present *The Conquest of Spain* to both formal and informal students of literature in the same way that we present the works of any respected playwright: in a convenient, accessible, modernized, annotated, standalone text. I am privileged to send this book into the world in honor of Mary Pix.

MARY PIX

THE CONQUEST OF SPAIN

Dramatis Personae

KING RHODERIQUE OF SPAIN
JULIANUS, a famed Spanish general
JACINCTA, daughter to Julianus, engaged to Theomantius
ANTONIO, nephew to Julianus
MARGARETTA, a noble orphan under the care of Julianus,
    privately married to Antonio
THEOMANTIUS, a Spanish noble, engaged to Jacincta and
    presumed dead
ALVAREZ, friend to Antonio
JAQUEZ, slave to Alvarez
CLOTHARIO, a lord
LODOVICUS, a lord
DON GOMEZ, a governor of a castle
MULLYMUMEN, general of the Moors

MOORS, OFFICERS, GUARDS, SOLDIERS, WOMEN,
ATTENDANTS, SERVANTS, COURTIERS, PRISONERS,
SLAVES

Prologue

How bold a venture does our author make! 1
And what strange measures to his wishes take!
How could he hope the tragic scene should please,
When art's a jest, and sense a loathed disease?
What prospect of advantage could he find 5
In the just painted passions of the mind
And the sublimer droughts of humankind?
Who listens now to nature's charming voice,
When all are pleased with empty show and noise,
Loud tumid bombast or low farce and dance: 10
The farfetched trash of Italy and France?
What various dishes for you have we dressed,
And what strange olios have set out our feast?
Yet these please now your vicious palates more
Than your wise sires the tragic muse of yore. 15
The tragic muse, the glory of our nation,
Is thrown aside, despised like an old fashion.
In vain with toil the artful bards have strove
Your fickle tastes to please and to improve.
All this our author knew, yet still would on 20
And tempt the dangers he was warned to shun.
No dire prediction could his mind depress,
And sure his courage merits some success.
Bravely resolved he does his sentence wait,
Nor dreads your frowns, nor would provoke your hate, 25
But owns your power, and hopes a prosperous fate.

2. his: The prologue uses male pronouns for Pix.
11. tumid bombast: swollen, elaborate language
13. olios: dishes of mixed-up ingredients
26. owns: acknowledges

Act I, Scene i

Scene: an antechamber in the court

Enter ANTONIO, MARGARETTA, *and* ALVAREZ

ANTONIO
Why dost thou sigh with this unusual care, 1
And grasp me with such eager fond concern
As if we never were to meet again?

MARGARETTA
Thus to be hurried from the feast of nature,
The downy peace of a retired life, 5
Here to be fixed at court, the place I hate,
To have my dearest lord summoned away
By honor's shrill commands, borne from my sight
To share impartial danger in the field,
I swear it is too much. Speak, Alvarez, 10
Thou faithful witness of our secret vows,
Are not these causes worthy of my grief?

ALVAREZ
I had rather play the woman and weep those tears
Than see them drown the luster of your eyes.

MARGARETTA
The wretched by complaint oft find relief, 15
But I have no such privilege in sorrow.
Though gnawing anguish prey upon my heart,
In public I must wear a face serene,
Stifle my rising sighs, restrain my tears,
And well dissemble all the pangs I feel, 20
Lest they betray our marriage.

---

11. secret vows: secret marriage
20. dissemble: conceal
21. betray: give away

ANTONIO
What shall I do to calm thy growing fears?

MARGARETTA
Nothing but stay. Do that, and I am blessed.
Leave the rough business of the dreadful war
To those inured to bloody fields of horror.   25
Thou wert not made for summer's scorching heats,
Nor winter's piercing cold and fatal damps;
Thou only wert designed for love and peace.
Honor and wealth already are your slaves,
Conquest has wreathed your brow with verdant laurels,   30
And Barcelona owns you for her lord.
What would you more? Alas! I fear
My humble fortunes drive you from my arms.

ANTONIO
Alvarez, hear you this? Oh, Margaretta!
Is there on earth a fortune worthy thee?   35
Thy virtues valued but at half their price
Would over buy the globe with all its glories.
Was not thy birth noble as Spain can boast?
Thy father loyal, generous, and valiant?
Who, when he had exhausted all his store   40
In grateful offices of public good,
The king confessed his merits, praised him much,
But found himself too poor to pay him back,
And, by delaying what was in his power,
Thy father, to his shame, died unrewarded.   45

MARGARETTA
And left me an unhappy, helpless orphan,

25. inured to: used to
30. verdant: green
31. owns: acknowledges
40. all his store: all his wealth
44-45. to his shame: perhaps the king's shame, or perhaps Margaretta's father's

Exposed to this unhospitable world.
But heaven was kind, for from my father's obsequies
Great Julianus led me to his palace
And bred me up with his own beauteous daughter.   50

ALVAREZ
And well you merited his pious care.

ANTONIO
Weep not, my love, let past afflictions die.
Load not thy memory with mournful thoughts.
When my great uncle's fame shall be rehearsed
In after times, in ages yet behind,   55
This one excelling act of guarding thee
Shall crown the immortal story.

MARGARETTA
My much-loved lord, my peace, my wish, my husband:
That dearest name sums all the joys of life.
Blessed be the hour, and blessed the holy priest   60
That joined our hands and sealed this happy contract.

ANTONIO
Thou dearest object of my doting heart!

ALVAREZ
Is wedlock stored with tenderness like this?
Who would not then be married!

ANTONIO
Kind Alvarez,   65
With well-pleased eyes thou viewest my lovely choice,
For thou art blessed Antonio's other treasure.

---

47. unhospitable: inhospitable
48. obsequies: funeral rites
51. merited: deserved
54. rehearsed: repeated

ALVAREZ
From laughing youth up to these busy years
Our souls have held the band of manly friendship.

ANTONIO
Never may time nor accident divide it. 70
My friend, my charming wife.

ALVAREZ
She is strangely beauteous.

ANTONIO
She is, Alvarez, and by heaven I swear
It glads me more to call this treasure mine
Than were I emperor of the world without her. 75
Oh, Margaretta! Couldst thou read my thoughts,
For 'tis not in the power of words to express them,
How constant, fond, entirely full of thee
They rise with eager transport in my soul,
By them alone thou'dst know how dear I hold thee. 80

MARGARETTA
Yet you will leave me to despair.

ANTONIO
But to defend my country from the Moors,
That I may long enjoy thy matchless beauty.

MARGARETTA
But Julianus!

ANTONIO
Fear not. He will forgive our secret marriage. 85

74. glads: pleases
75. Than were I: Than if I were
76. Couldst thou: If you could
78. fond: simple, foolish
83. That I may: So that I may

THE CONQUEST OF SPAIN

ALVAREZ
Though at this time, when war looks red upon us,
It is not fit to tell him tales of love,
Yet when soft peace ensues, he'll crown your wishes.

MARGARETTA
Antonio is his favorite near allied,
And by expiring parents left his charge.   90
I know, my lord, the general is good,
But he designs you for some happier maid:
One to whom fortune, with a partial hand,
Has given
The shining mass which she had long been gathering   95
From lavish epicurus and thoughtless heirs.

ANTONIO
For Margaretta, I condemn it all
And count it dross when balanced with thy worth.

MARGARETTA
Oh! How my boding heart does beat and ache,
Reflecting on the hazards thou must run: 100
Dangers which threatens life and dearer love:
Love, which is grown the precious vital heat
Essential to this little tender frame,
And both must live, or both decay together.

ANTONIO
Thou soft delight, the music of whose voice   105
Runs to my heart and brings new raptures there,
Tell me what I shall say to charm thy cares.

88. crown: endorse, praise
90. And by...charge: And was left by dying parents in Julianus' care
93. partial: biased
96. epicures: ones who love good food and drink
98. dross: trash
98. balanced: compared
103. tender frame: Margaretta's body
107. charm thy cares: dismiss your fears

MARGARETTA
Swear that neither fate nor ill-timed chance
Shall change your love and dear prized faith to me.
Swear, that I may preserve the pleasing oath   110
And when you're gone repeat it to my heart.

ANTONIO
By all our ecstasies already past,
By all our boundless pleasures yet to come,
By the dear unborn pledge of joy thou bearest,
My soul shall never know another flame,   115
Never incline to an inconstant wish,
Nor my eyes stay to gaze on any object
But thy dear world of beauties.

MARGARETTA
Enough, my soul's at ease, and doubt is lost.

[*Trumpets sound*]

ALVAREZ
Hark! The trumpets speak the king at hand.   120
This morning Julianus takes his leave.

ANTONIO
To win new trophies for the inglorious king,
Who wastes his life in luxury and ease.

MARGARETTA
Lose not a thought on him; love all exacts:
He bids us husband the dear little stock   125
Which yet is left to bless our eager wishes.
Come, let us give the few remaining minutes
To faithful tenderness and soft farewells.

110. preserve: save, remember
114. pledge of joy: a baby. (Margaretta is pregnant.)
123-126. love all exacts…wishes: Love requires everything and would have us tend to the little time we have left together.

Let not the smallest part of scanty time
Fleet by, unknowing of our mutual joys, 130
Till that unhappy crisis which divides us.

ANTONIO [*holding her*]
Thus to my heart forever could I hold thee,
To glory deaf, regardless of a name,
Neglecting honor and despising fame.

Exeunt ANTONIO *and* MARGARETTA

ALVAREZ
What mean these warring passions in my breast? 135
Honor, love, friendship, fury, and despair,
Ye legion of tormentors, how you rack me!
Yet I will struggle with this mighty tumult.
Honor, what art thou but an idle dream,
A gaudy bauble chased by beardless boys, 140
Which, when we catch, proves nothing but opinion?
Love, thou indeed art an essential blessing:
The unexhausted source of all our pleasures.
Why then should friendship's barren name forbid thee?
What is a friend but one who shares in common 145
The advantages of life with him he loves?
And marriage is engrossing to himself.
Antonio then dissolves the band, not I.
Oh! Margaretta! I must and will enjoy thee.
Jaquez, my faithful slave, where art thou? 150

Enter JAQUEZ

JAQUEZ
Where I have overheard all, and come prepared.

133. name: reputation
138. tumult: confusion
140: bauble: toy, trinket, or decoration; in the 1705 edition, "bubble"
147. is engrossing to himself: takes up all of Antonio's attention
148. the band: (of friendship)

ALVAREZ
Long have I found thee diligent and subtle,
And I have great occasion for those qualities.
I am in love.

JAQUEZ
With lord Antonio's wife.   155

ALVAREZ
Confusion blast that title! 'Tis my bane.
Couldst thou no other way distinguish her
But by the only sound I would forget?

JAQUEZ
Thus warned, I'll be more careful.

ALVAREZ
Fond Alvarez!   160
Why dost thou blush to think upon the sin
Thou darest resolve to act? 'Tis coward villainy.

JAQUEZ
You are much disturbed.

ALVAREZ
Aided by thee, all will again be well.
Anon we march against the sooty Moors.   165
Be it thy care to intercept all letters
That pass between Antonio and that lady.
'Tis easy to be done as I'll direct thee.
I have a half formed thought, which, well improved,
Will ease my longing soul. But see, the king.   170
Let us withdraw, where we may think on it farther.

Exeunt

153. occasion: need
156. that title: "wife"
160. Fond: simple, foolish
165. Anon: soon, at once
166. thy care: your job

Act I, Scene ii

Enter KING, CLOTHARIO, *and* LODOVICUS.
GUARDS *and* COURTIERS *at a distance.*

KING
This day great Julianus leads to war,
Which swells my hopes of victory and love.
Though our young warriors have with loss been foiled,
Now he consents to lead, our cares are fled.
What are these Moors, that they should make us fear? 5
A straggling crew, unskilled in Spanish discipline.
Our well-tried soldiers soon will cut them off
And raze the memory of this invasion.
Then let it not disturb our royal thoughts;
Certain of conquest, I give loose to pleasure. 10
Clothario and Lodovicus, be you employed
To see the court shine like another paradise;
Let every sense be feasted with delight.

LODOVICUS
First let the general be farther off.
Your majesty well knows he frowns on vanity; 15
His soul was stamped of the old Roman make:
Stern valor and strict virtue are his pleasures,
His only study how he may restore
The ancient, awful dignity of Spain.
Both mind and body join to furnish out 20
A rough, unpolished, perfect soldier.

KING
Such indeed he is, yet from him came
The softest creature nature ever made.

---

4. Now he consents: Now that he consents
4. cares: worries
10. give loose: give way, indulge
16. His soul...make: His soul is made in the same fashion as the old Romans.
20. furnish out: complete, complement

Fool that thou art to talk of Julianus
When all my thoughts are busy with Jacincta. 25
Let the old man amidst his iron warriors
Make long harangues and win the soldiers' hearts
Whilst with his beauteous daughter I am blessed,
Lost in the revels of tumultuous joy.

CLOTHARIO
Alas! My gracious sovereign, I fear 30
You'll find it hard to work her to your purpose.
Her father's steady virtue is her guide,
And she, with early piety, improves
The rules by which the holy vestals walk.

LODOVICUS
Her actions and her words are all divine, 35
As if from her new sectaries were to rise
And new discoveries of worlds above,
She, the fair saint, to lead the shining way
And charm us with her beauty to pursue.

KING
Ha! Traitors! Dare you talk 40
To me? Dare you do this, now, when I range
Warm in the dear pursuit of wanton bliss?
Hence from my sight, ye useless dregs of vice.
Have you so long been slaves to my desires,
And do you now forget your humble business? 45
When I have named the object of my wishes,
Your diligence should still supply the means.

---

27. harangues: speeches
33. improves: raises the bar for
36. sectaries: sects
42. wanton: careless
45. your humble business: your responsibilities
47. still: always

CLOTHARIO
Jacincta's yours, though she be chaste as Lucrece,
Beyond what lovers think or poets feign.
Your youth and majesty have charms sufficient   50
To melt the frozen zone and reach her heart.

LODOVICUS
Showing the difficulty to obtain,
We but enhance the value of the prize.
She shall be yours, that lovely dazzling beauty
To which not Spain, nor all the world besides,   55
Can find a parallel. Believe her gained.

KING
Ay, now you speak like men resolved to rise
And shine the envy of the gazing court,
Wear all the gaudy honors I can give,
But live dependent on my pleasures.   60

CLOTHARIO
See, the general.

Enter JULIANUS, JACINCTA, MARGARETTA,
ANTONIO, ALVAREZ, WOMEN *and* OFFICERS

KING
Welcome, thou guardian genius of my throne,
My general, my father and my friend.
Safety and peace come with thee, cheerful triumph
Waits with impatience to reward thy labors.   65
Proclaim a jubilee through all our cities.
Great Julianus comes! Be that the shout

48. Lucrece: a Roman noblewoman renowned for her honor, who killed herself after being raped by the king's son
56. Believe her gained: Believe that she is yours.
57. to rise: (politically)
60. dependent on my pleasures: according to my desires
62. genius: supernatural protector, guardian angel

From whose blessed echo Spain with joy receives
The pleasing omen of assured success.

JULIANUS
Whither does all of this wondrous goodness lead? 70
You call the mantling blood into my face
And make me young again in spite of nature.
Such power has condescending majesty.

KING
Forgive me, soldier, that in erring youth
I left neglected thy superior virtue. 75
Now I embrace thee as the prop of empire.

JULIANUS
Thus warmed, command me quickly to the fight.
Old as I am, I shall make work among them
That with whole hecatombs of sunburnt Moors
I may repay this and deserve your praise. 80

KING
Victory cannot fail; your beauteous daughter
Carries eternal conquest in her eyes.
Again our court shall boast and vie with France
For soft prevailing charms. That other fair one
Methinks I have seen before. 85

JULIANUS
The lovely daughter
Of brave Antigones. Nay, think not, courtiers,
A worthier man never adorned the world.
Had he been yet alive, or such as he,
Spain ne'er had heard of Mullymumen's name. 90
'Tis from our wantonness, our slothful ease,

---

71. mantling: covering
79. hecatombs: in Greece, a large sacrifice of cattle
87. Antigones: Margaretta's father, perhaps "Antigonos" or "Antigonus"

THE CONQUEST OF SPAIN

From our neglect of arms, the Moors presume
Thus to defy us at our very gates.
Your pardon, shining things, if I am too rough,
For I have not been used to courts of late. 95
My soldiers only will remember me,
And them I shall know how to entertain.

KING
Thou loyal, mighty pillar of my state!
Speak: hast thou nothing to request of me
Before the great decisive day? 100

JULIANUS
It was your pleasure
That I should leave safe in your kingly trust
All that my heart held dear. The gracious offer
Has eased my soul of many anxious thought.
My castle stands so near the enemy 105
That, had I placed them there as I designed,
The hated noise of war, the rude confusion,
Dreadful to virgin ears, the shrieks of cowards,
The cries and hollow groans of dying men
Had pierced their gentle natures. With you secure 110
They may at ease expect the great event.
Here, royal sir, take this: my poor Jacincta,
And this: the daughter of my good old friend,
Equally dear to Julianus' breast.
With you I leave them, and from your hands again 115
At my return shall ask the sacred pledges.

KING
As life and empire will thy king preserve them.

---

106. them: Jacincta and Margaretta
110. had pierced: would have pierced
111. expect the great event: wait out the fighting
113. And this: Margaretta
116. shall ask the sacred pledges: will request them back again
117. As life and empire: As carefully as my own life and kingdom

But will not fair Jacincta speak to us?
For we delight to hear her pleasing words.

JULIANUS
A sable cloud of grief hangs o'er her thoughts,   120
For she has lost in this unhappy war
A lover, which we all have cause to mourn.
Blush not, my girl, he well deserved thy heart
And was thy father's choice, whose mind, exempt
From the soft bias of thy tender passion,   125
Examined him with reason's wary eye
And found him truly perfect.

KING
Theomantius?

JULIANUS
The same. I loved the noble, warlike youth
And should not easily forgive my daughter   130
Could she so soon forget him.

KING
The maid that loves a soldier, fair Jacincta,
Must arm herself against the lot of battle:
There, death and glory hold the doubtful scale,
And oft with thoughtless haste blind chance decides   135
The hero falls, and the chill coward's spared.
None but your powerful father ever knew
To fix the giddy wheel: fortune's his slave.

JACINCTA
Grant it, ye powers.

---

119. we: the pronoun used by royalty
124. And was thy father's choice: And had my support
133. Must arm herself...battle: Must prepare herself for the risks that battle brings
137. ever knew: ever knew how
138. To fix the giddy wheel: To freeze or control the wheel of fortune

THE CONQUEST OF SPAIN

KING
If heaven views you but with my regard, 140
Ask what you will, you cannot be denied.

JACINCTA
One small request, great sir, I have to you,
That in my father's absence I have leave
To live recluse, unseeing and unseen,
Where I may pass my melancholy hours 145
In tears and vows, such as my fate requires.

KING
Choose your apartment in our royal palace,
And no rude breath shall break the hallowed air
Made sacred to yourself and this bright virgin,
The soft companion of your solitude. 150
There live like pious maids in silent cloisters,
Till the loud trumpets and repeated shouts
Proclaim the general's victory and return,
And call you forth.

JULIANUS
This most indulgent goodness 155
Shows you the best of men as well as kings.
Yes, doubt not conquest when I'm thus prepared.
By heaven, I'm fired, eager for the war
As when at first, in the high rage of youth,
I chased immortal fame. Draw up your troops, 160
Antonio; what, unplumed? This is not well.
Thou art a soldier, and soldiers should be forward.
I tell thee, lord, I went not with more joy
Unto my maiden bride that hymen night,
From whence I gained this jewel of my heart, 165

140. with my regard: as I do
151. pious maids in silent cloisters: nuns
158. fired: fired up, excited
161. what, unplumed?: Antonio is not dressed for battle
164. hymen night: wedding night

Than now I do unto my second nuptials.
Honor: oh, she's a gallant mistress.

ANTONIO
Ever young.
Think not, my lord, that I am unprepared,
A trifling laggard in the glorious race: 170
When such I am, disown me of your blood,
And hold me most unworthy your esteem.

JULIANUS
Gallant Antonio!

ANTONIO
Led on by you,
We shall find business for the Africans. 175

KING
They'll curse the ambition that betrayed them to you.

JULIANUS
This honor, which your majesty has given me,
Though better it might fit another's wearing,
Whose able limbs time has not yet contracted,
Nor half so many winters quenched his blood, 180
Yet, like a spring, it has revived again
This autumn of my years. Let us away:
We will destroy this swarthy brood of hell,
Dispatch them with such momentary slaughter
That late posterity shall doubt the legend 185
And only think their old forefathers dreamt.

KING
My friend, my godlike hero, sound to march.

---

172. hold me: consider me
175. find business: literally, give them something to do, keep them busy
185. late posterity: future generations

Even we ourselves mean to conduct you forward
And view the cheerful soldiers with what joy
They wait your wished approach. Come on, my general;   190
Sound all the martial instruments of war
That as we pass, your souls may fire.

Trumpets sound and drums beat.
KING *going*, JACINCTA *kneels to* KING

JACINCTA
Dread sovereign,
If in your eyes Jacincta has found grace,
Forgive the female weakness of my mind: 195
My father bred me up with tenderest care
And still preserved me from the threatening storms
Of life's unruly tempest, safe and happy;
Beneath his sheltering wing my fears were hushed,
Nor looked I farther, till, by his command,   200
I loved the noble copy of himself,
My Theomantius. Oh, untimely fate!
This cruel war has cropped his hopeful bloom
And thrown him pale and withered to his grave.
This I have learned to bear, yet more I'll try,   205
And since 'tis now decreed I must resign
The only refuge of my trembling youth,
Give me a moment's leave to weigh the hazard,
The certain danger and uncertain safety,
To hang about his knees and tell my sorrows,   210
To beg paternal blessings ere he goes,
With fondness much unfit for many eyes.

KING
Take your request, and all with me retire.
Only remember, valiant Julianus,

197. still: always
201. the noble copy of himself: perhaps, "another soldier"
203. cropped: cut down
207. The only refuge of my trembling youth: Julianus

That every minute's stay is robbed from fame. 215

JULIANUS
Oh, do not think that I will loiter here.
A short farewell, a blessing on my children,
And I am gone swift as your own desires.

Exeunt KING *and* COURTIERS [*all but*
JULIANUS, JACINCTA, *and* MARGARETTA]

JULIANUS
What wouldst thou now, thou darling of my age,
Thou loved resemblance of thy charming mother? 220
And thou, fair Margaretta? Speak your wishes,
And share a father's and a friend's affection.

JACINCTA
The first dear suit that rises to my tongue,
Preferred to all the rest, is your own life.
Be careful of yourself, or I am lost. 225

JULIANUS
I'll take a soldier's care, I do assure thee:
Foremost to charge and cautious to retreat;
Watchful to take advantage of the enemy
And active to employ the opportunity;
Well to command and careful to advise, 230
That I may merit what a general should,
And then I dare trust fortune with the rest.
Why dost thou weep, my lovely, drooping charge?
Come, I have guessed the cause of thy concern.
Thou fearest for a young soldier, or I err. 235
Dwells not Antonio in those fears?

MARGARETTA
My lord.

223. suit: request

THE CONQUEST OF SPAIN

JULIANUS
Nay, no excuse. That blush confirms my thoughts.
But oh! Fair maid, beware the wiles of love;
Trust not too easily to faithless men.   240
Indeed, Antonio is a worthy lord,
But he is young, and his possessions large:
All means for riot, if he bends that way.
Thou art descended from as glorious ancestors;
Then let not wealth, titles, nor pomp betray thee   245
To stain the ancient honor of thy race.

MARGARETTA
Heaven forbid!

JULIANUS
Forgive me, Margaretta,
Old men will claim a privilege to talk.
Only be cautious. 'Tis a dangerous world,   250
And youth and beauty are the common wrack.
Let virtue be thy guide, and thou art safe.
Trust me, I love thee as my child.

MARGARETTA
My father,
For so I have ever found you, kind and good,
You seem inclined to chide my guilty weakness.   255
How have I erred, how failed in my obedience?

JULIANUS
No, thou art innocent as infant angels,
Dear to my bosom as my own Jacincta.
Nor is the youth less loved, but I observed
Thy charming eyes fixed mutually on his,   260
Shoot all their fires there, and melt when he withdrew:
Perhaps 'twas only friendship. I have done.

---

243. means for riot: tools for recklessness
245. let not wealth...betray thee: do not be tempted by wealth or titles
251. wrack: wreck, disaster
262. I have done: I am finished.

The fleeting minutes pass, and I lose time.
What is it my Jacincta has to say?

JACINCTA
Oh, sir, if you will but with patience hear me, 265
I have a tale to unfold concerns you nearly:
A gloomy fear that hangs upon my soul,
And every peaceful faculty distracts.

JULIANUS
I am surprised! But tell me what thou meanest.

JACINCTA
Look kindly, then, and promise to forgive me. 270

JULIANUS
Fear not, Jacincta.

JACINCTA
Call to your noble mind
The struggling grief of your unhappy child
When you talked of leaving me at court.

JULIANUS
I well remember thy incessant tears 275
When the repeated royal mandates came,
But then it was we first received the news
Of Theomantius's death.

JACINCTA
The lovely youth
Not all my sorrows can enough lament. 280
Alas! I had resolved to mourn his loss
In lonely shades and unfrequented groves,
To waste my wretched days in sad despair,
Counting the tedious minutes with my sighs.

266. concerns: that concerns

JULIANUS
And raging war has broke this mournful scene. 285
Is not that all?

JACINCTA
Oh, no, my dearest father,
But your severer virtue awes my words.
Fain I would tell you all yet want the power;
Blushing confusion chokes the hated tale, 290
And shame o'erspreads my face as I were guilty
When I would blame another.

JULIANUS
What sayest thou?
But surely I am wide of truth.

JACINCTA
The king. 295

JULIANUS
Stop thou there, Jacincta, as thou lovest thy father,
Nor with thy idle fears disturb my soul
Because he condescended to regard
Thy little portion of unartful beauty.
Interpret not his praise to thy dishonor. 300
Perhaps thou hast heard some murmurers defame him;
To me they would have railed, but I was deaf;
Honor forbid that I should listen to them.
Shake off these doubts, have nobler thoughts, my child;
Revere the royal man thy father serves. 305

JACINCTA
But yet my lord.

289. Fain: Gladly
289. want: lack
291. as I were: as if I were
294. I am wide of truth: my guess is wrong.
299. unartful: either "simple" or "natural"
302. I was deaf: I refused to listed

JULIANUS

No more, I charge you, of this fond mistake.
Does he not trust me with unbounded power?
With the united force of all his kingdoms?
And can he mean me ill? 310

JACINCTA

I'll urge no farther,
Only to heaven direct my humble prayers:
Protect my father, give him victory,
And save my innocence.

MARGARETTA

With equal zeal I offer my petitions: 315
Bestow, ye great disposers of our fate,
Long life and endless joy on Julianus.
Shower all your blessings on his reverend head,
And guard him back with honor, peace, and safety.

JULIANUS

I go, my children, with assured success. 320
The noble cause I wear upon my sword
Is of itself sufficient to prevail.
Justice and piety fight on our sides;
Against such odds, who dare dispute the field?
One chaste embrace, and then farewell. 325

JACINCTA

Yet stay.
One moment longer stay and bless my eyes.
When that's expired, I will surmount my fears
And calmly part.

JULIANUS

The sacred powers are just, 330

---

307. fond: foolish
311. urge: push it
314. innocence: chastity
328. When that's expired: After that moment

THE CONQUEST OF SPAIN

And in the course of many rolling years,
No horrid sin starts up to blast my hopes,
No vile offense vexes my memory,
And honest men are heaven's peculiar care.
Why art thou sad? 335

JACINCTA
Oh! You have manly courage,
But I, of gentler mold, was made a woman:
My eyes run o'er, and my full heart presages
We ne'er shall meet in happiness again.

JULIANUS
All groundless. I tell thee, my Jacincta, 340
Our greatest ills of life ourselves create:
Our anxious care, our follies, and our fondness
Ever betray us to a thousand dangers,
And humankind are still their own undoers.
Be thou upright, and then suspect no harm. 345
By heaven! I prattle thus, forgetting honor.
But thou art dear to me as peace or glory;
The vital blood that circles round my heart
Is not one half so precious. Banish thy scruples.

JACINCTA
My godlike father, kind as providence, 350
Who views our faults with a forgiving eye,
Hears us repine with ceaseless discontent
Yet still continues its unwearied goodness.
But I'll no longer hold you from your warriors,
Farewell. 355

---

332. my hopes: (of heaven)
334. peculiar: special
338. presages: predicts
343: Ever: Always
349. scruples: fears
350-353. My godlike father...unwearied goodness: That is, Julianus, like God, has ungrateful children but is always good to them.

JULIANUS

Why dost thou damp the few remaining sparkles
That faintly warm my age with dying vigor?
Why dost thou wound my soul with boding words
And with thy streaming tears make parting dreadful?
Farewell to both, and the blessed gods protect you. 360

Exit

JACINCTA

He's gone, and gloomy terror fills my mind.
Come, my fair friend, let us begin our task,
Fly all delight and all society,
Resolve to live in this distressed court
Silent and sad as death. 365

MARGARETTA

I meet your wishes.
Oh, love! Thou pleasing solitude of mind,
Thou spacious field of fancy, beauteous prospect,
Where tender jealousies and gentle raptures,
And hopes and fears, desires and endless joys 370
Compose the soft variety of life.

JACINCTA

Sure 'twas the business of some guardian angel
To fit our hearts for such entire sympathy.
Let us be gone; I long to indulge my grief:
My father's danger and my lover's fate: 375
What greater woes can angry powers create?

Exeunt

End of Act I

---

358. boding: ill-boding
363. Fly: Hide from

Act II, Scene i

[Scene: inside the castle]

Enter KING, CLOTHARIO, *and* LODOVICUS

LODOVICUS
Give her but time to think, and she'll comply. 1

KING
Oh! Never. With strong aversion and severe disdain
She flies my love, and leaves no glimpse of hope.
Late, as I gently pressed on her retirement
And urged my tale of irresistless passion, 5
With frowning scorn and firmest resolution,
Even such as shows she is not to be moved,
The cruel fair repulsed my eager fires.

CLOTHARIO
When amorous night and gentle silence reigned,
Inspiring soft desires and tender wishes, 10
When pride and reason, careless of their charge,
Nodded a while and left the maid defenseless,
Could she refuse your majesty?

KING
Refuse!
The word's too mild: abhor, detest, and loathe. 15
Oh! She is fair and sweet as springing flowers,
But cold and charit'less as winter frosts.
What shall I do? I burn, and I despair:
I cannot wait a tedious hated siege;
My fierce desire is too impatient grown. 20

1. her: Jacincta
4. Late: Recently
5. irresistless: irresistible
11. careless of their charge: forgetting their responsibilities
12. Nodded: Slept

Her father may return, or she may fly.

CLOTHARIO
The last I shall be watchful to prevent.
And might I be permitted to advise,
Seize on the prey while yet 'tis in your power,
For opportunity is a captious goddess: 25
If once neglected, she returns no more.

KING
Thou counselest well. By heaven it shall be so;
I will possess in spite of all her hate:
Snatch the coy charmer to my longing arms,
Deaf to her prayers as she has been to mine. 30

LODOVICUS
Yet if I may be heard, forbear a while;
Think on the event, on her stern father's power.
I fear not for Jacincta, but—

KING
For thyself.
Be dumb, thou coward, spare thy idle breath. 35
As well thou may'st restrain the flowing tide,
Command the fire, and control the wind,
As once delay the action I have purposed.

LODOVICUS
I have done, and have resolved to assist your pleasure.

CLOTHARIO
When once enjoyed, your majesty will find 40
The bright Jacincta lay by all her rage,

22. The last: The latter
25. captious: critical
30. Deaf to her prayers: Ignoring her pleas
31. forbear: hold off, wait
35. dumb: silent

THE CONQUEST OF SPAIN

Her rigid coldness and her virgin fears,
And pay her grateful offerings to love.
Oh! She will put on all her melting softness,
And practice every subtle female art 45
To fix you ever her imperial lover.

KING
That I much doubt, but be it as it will,
I'll sum up all my joys, and with full transport,
In one luxurious hour possess the whole.
Say the rich feast should never be renewed, 50
Yet the remembrance still shall bless my soul;
The thinking faculty shall be indulged,
And I'll repeat the pleasure to my heart,
Till even desire be satiated.

LODOVICUS
Yet I am lost 55
To think how this may be with secrecy.

KING
Dull as thou art, dost thou pretend to thought?
Assist, ye slaves, and act as I command,
Nor strain your poor inventions any farther.
'Tis requisite the beauteous friends be parted. 60
Tell them that all the court repine to see
Their noble births thus peevishly forgot,
Their youthful charms thus shrouded in despair.
Tell them, it is of moment to my honor
That they admit the state due to their quality. 65
Say anything may tempt them to comply,

---

46. imperial: kingly
48. with full transport: forgetting myself
50. renewed: repeated
59. inventions: plots
60. requisite: necessary
61. repine: regret, disapprove
64. moment: importance

And if they still refuse, part them by force.
Clothario, thou art keeper of this tower,
Which long has served my amorous purposes;
Thither convey Jacincta. For the other, 70
Confine her where she is.

CLOTHARIO
We shall observe, and readily obey.

KING
In the meantime, I will ascend the tower,
From whence I may discern the distant camp
And guess imperfectly how they succeed. 75
But fly and bring my bright Jacincta here.
Let heroes mind the business of the war;
To love and to possess is all my care.

Exeunt severally

---

69. amorous purposes: affairs
70. Thither convey: There take
74. the distant camp: (of the soldiers)
78. all my care: all I care about

Act II, Scene ii

Enter JACINCTA *and* MARGARETTA

JACINCTA
Thus like the children of despair and horror, 1
Weeping and trembling, hopeless of success,
We walk the mournful limits of our prison:
For now we are confined with locks and bars,
Perhaps designed a sacrifice to violence; 5
Since I refused the tyrant's impious love,
Who knows what black revenge he may pursue?
Oh! Margaretta, I am lost forever.
This I foresaw, but could not be believed:
My dearest father, in himself too honest 10
E'er to suspect another of such villainy,
Was deaf to my complaint and chid my fears.

MARGARETTA
Let not your soul resign itself to sorrow,
For we are guards to one another still.
The king, if ill inclined, which heaven forbid, 15
Yet dares not openly pursue his guilt.
In these tumultuous times, it might be fatal
To add one crime to his polluted life.

JACINCTA
Thou, my fair friend, art all the guide I've left,
And what art thou 'gainst arbitrary power? 20
Yet it is possible we may be safe.
Oh! Theomantius, dost thou know my grief?
Sure if thou dost, 'twill interrupt thy joy;
The chaste, the endless truth I've vowed thy memory,
The spotless honor I've preserved from childhood, 25

---

5. designed: prepared as
16. his guilt: his evil goal
17. fatal: fatal to his soul
23. thy joy: that is, in heaven

All, all is now in danger.

Enter LODOVICUS *and* CLOTHARIO

CLOTHARIO
Hail ye bright ornaments of our happy court,
Ye lovely miracles of human race,
Modest as infant nature in her bloom,
And fair as the inhabitants of heaven. 30
The king is still in search and longs to find
New ways to do our mighty general honor;
Apartments by his royal will assigned,
Rich with the wealthy spoil of ransacked nations,
And crowds of kneeling slaves wait your approach. 35

LODOVICUS
The Tyrian purple and the Indian gold,
Curiously interwove by artful hands,
Large Orient pearl, and gems of highest value,
Inferior only to your radiant eyes,
Are placed in beauteous order all around, 40
While gentle harmony exerts its power
To waft celestial strains worthy your welcome.

JACINCTA
For whom is this fine pageantry designed?
It was my father's will, and my request,
That free from flatterers, from noise and show, 45
Our silent hours might pass till his return.
I prithee go, and from the common herd
Choose some vain thing that may affect such trifles;
Leave us our humble choice.

33. will: decision, decree
35. wait your approach: await you
42. worthy: worthy of
47. the common herd: the commoners
48. vain thing: shallow and superficial person, worthless person
48. affect: desire, enjoy

CLOTHARIO
To chide the officious servants of your pleasure 50
Is something hard, and suits not with your goodness;
But beauty hath a privilege to frown.
The fiery warrior, and the sage philosopher,
The ambitious monarch, all submit to beauty
And yield their reason to your soft command. 55

LODOVICUS
Oh, they are formed for universal sway,
The source of joy, and idols of the world.

MARGARETTA
Whither does this fine oratory tend?
On us 'tis lost. We wish to be alone.

CLOTHARIO
We have received command from the king 60
To wait you to your several apartments,
For so his sacred majesty ordains.

JACINCTA
Ha! Part us! No, that you shall never do;
We have resolved to bear our woes together.
Both love and misery have made us one: 65
The soul and body not more closely joined;
Be sure when we are separate, we die.

MARGARETTA
We want no state, no vain destructive honor;
Content with privacy, we shun the crowd,

---

50. officious: dutiful
51. hard: cruel
56. they: beautiful women (Jacincta and Margaretta)
58. Wither...tend?: Where is all this fine speech leading?
61. wait you: take you
61. several: separate
68. state: honors

Busy attendance, and deluding pomp; 70
Tumult and noise is what we most abhor.

CLOTHARIO
The mighty Rhoderique, whose word is power,
Commands that fair Jacincta straight remove
Where all things fitting her high dignity,
Enough to vie with haughty Eastern queens, 75
Fair noble maids, titles and laughing joy
Attend her.

JACINCTA
Here will I stay, 'twas here my father left me.

LODOVICUS
'Tis dangerous to listen to your words.

JACINCTA
Oh my heart! 80
What can you mean? You will not force me hence.

MARGARETTA
Your forms are human and your souls immortal.
Away; 'tis most unmanly.

LODOVICUS
You're too fearful;
Believe me, madam, there's no ill intended. 85
The king designs much good and many favors
To raise your beauty and your father's valor.
Who waits there? Where are those dependent slaves?
Conduct that lady as you are ordered.

Enter SERVANTS

71. Tumult: Commotion
73. straight remove: immediately go
82. Your forms are human and your souls immortal: an indirect threat: "you will one day die and answer for your sins"
86. designs: intends

THE CONQUEST OF SPAIN

JACINCTA
Hold! 90
Oh! For a dagger and a Roman courage!
Why are we taught self murder is a crime
Then, when the virgin hath no other refuge?

MARGARETTA
Ah! Whither do they drag my dear Jacincta?

JACINCTA
Oh! Margaretta! 'Tis in vain to weep. 95
If thou darest do a noble friendly part,
Snatch a villain's sword and strike me through,
For there is far less terror in that thought
Than what I now expect.

MARGARETTA
Gentle, blessed, abhorred, relentless villains! 100
Will nothing move your hearts?

JACINCTA
'Tis all in vain,
Yet I will shake the palace with my cries.
I may be heard; there is a power can save me,
At whose command the subtle lightning flies, 105
The thunder roars, and trembling earth gapes wide;
Either of these would save me from undoing.
Oh blast the tyrant, tear him, let him sink,
And free me from these fears.

MARGARETTA
Oh! My Jacincta! My dear suffering friend! 110

JACINCTA
Farewell.

91. a Roman courage: the courage to kill oneself
96. friendly part: favor
107. Either of these: thunder & lighting or an earthquake

MARGARETTA
Inhuman monsters, fiends of hell,
Better the Moors should be our lords than you;
Heaven's severest justice overtake you;
War, fire, famine, and contagious plagues,   115
Combined together in one mighty curse
Fall on this barbarous infernal race.
Be this no more a court, nor Spain a kingdom,
But gloomy death and desolation reign.

Exit JACINCTA, *forced off*
[*by* SERVANTS *and* CLOTHARIO]

LODOVICUS
Have peace, here violence is ended, you are safe.   120

MARGARETTA
Away, 'tis false, there is no safety here.

LODOVICUS
There is no end of women's fruitless rage,
Therefore I go; this apartment is your bounds.

Exit

MARGARETTA
There's nothing mine but sorrow.
Here will I lie and meditate a while   125
On all the various ills that rend my heart.
    (*Lies down*)
Let the rude slaves tread o'er me if they please,
Trample me, kill me, death is now my choice,
Lest I should live to prove Jacincta's wrongs.
My lord Antonio; why hast thou forgot me?   130

---

123. your bounds: the limits of your space (your prison)
126. rend: tear
127. rude slaves: ignorant villains
129. to prove: to confirm

THE CONQUEST OF SPAIN

Where are the expected couriers which were promised,
To bring me hourly news of thy dear safety?
Methinks I seem neglected and forsaken.
Warm in the youthful chase of dazzling glory,
Thou hast not leisure to remember me.　　　　　　　　　135
Oh, didst thou know what injuries live here,
Thou wouldst resign thy plumes and fight no more.
Why talk I thus? When thou perhaps art dead.
Would I could sleep, for thinking will distract me.

Enter JAQUEZ

JAQUEZ (*aside*)
With industry, a villain's useful quality,　　　　　　　　　140
I have found the fair one out.
Ye juster powers, when all the world's in joy,
When victory gilds our arms and bids us smile,
Do I behold the wife of great Antonio
Thus prostrate!　　　　　　　　　145

MARGARETTA
Ha! Do I not know that voice,
And did it not pronounce Antonio's name?
Jaquez, say, is my lord victorious?
Hath he received no hurt, and is he cheerful?
Oh! Let me ask a thousand thousand questions,　　　　　　　　　150
Impatient to be satisfied at once,
Yet not allow thee any time to answer.
But tell me, is he well?

JAQUEZ
In perfect health.

MARGARETTA
Then I am satisfied; the rest at leisure.　　　　　　　　　155

137. resign thy plums: put away your helmet
140. industry: cleverness
155. at leisure: in time, at your own pace

JAQUEZ
Though yet we cannot boast entire conquest,
We have gained many advantages of the enemy:
From the famed castle of renowned Don Gomez
This morn the youthful soldiers sallied forth
Under the lord Antonio's loved command. 160

MARGARETTA
Oh! My heart beats.

JAQUEZ
So looked the god of war
When Venus self adorned him for the field.
Such were his charms: the gems that decked his helmet
Seemed from his sparkling eyes to borrow luster; 165
Courage and happy conduct crowned his wishes,
And he returned successful.

MARGARETTA
Joyful sound!

JAQUEZ
Fifteen waving flags borne from the foe,
A thousand sooty prisoners bound in chains, 170
Who with their sullen looks and gnashing teeth
Expressed the innate malice of their souls,
These graced the triumph of the glorious youth.
Treble the number in the skirmish fell
And with the spoil rejoiced the soldiers' hearts. 175

MARGARETTA
Now blessings on thy tongue for this glad news.
Oh! My Jacincta! Angels protect thy virtue.
A little anxious space of time, and then
Our godlike conquerors will set us free.

---

163. Venus self adorned him: Venus herself dressed him
166. crowned: blessed, rewarded
174. Treble: Triple

JAQUEZ
The noble governor, who stands in fame 180
Next Julianus, the most worthy man
Our kingdom boasts, has one only daughter,
Gay as the spring, and fair as newborn light,
With all her charms she met the lord Antonio;
Six beauteous virgins bore her shining train, 185
And six preceding hailed him from their mistress,
Strowing with fragrant roses all the way.

MARGARETTA
'Twas wondrous kind. Eternal joy be with her.
Tell me her name, that I may know to bless it
For those dear honors which she gave my lord. 190

JAQUEZ
Delia. I could be lavish in her praise,
But your surprising charms restrain my language,
Excelling her as far.

MARGARETTA
Flatterer! But proceed.

JAQUEZ
Her snowy hand a laurel crown presented, 195
Which, kneeling, he as gracefully received.
Great Julianus and her father smiled,
While echoing voices through the palace rang
The pleasing names of Delia and Antonio.

MARGARETTA
'Tis well; but I grow sick and would retire. 200
What letters hast thou brought me from my lord?

180. governor: Don Gomez
181. Next: Next to, just after
187. Strowing: Strewing
191. lavish: liberal
200. retire: turn in

JAQUEZ (*aside*)
'Tis right; an angry blush has dyed her cheeks,
And rage is in her eyes.

MARGARETTA
Why dost thou pause?

JAQUEZ
Because I have no letter nor no message. 205
But 'twas his haste, and therefore most excusable.
He dispatched me to the king and had not time
To think.

MARGARETTA
How! Not of me! Oh, thou dost wrong him much.
I am his hourly thought, and he is mine, 210
Else I were most miserable.

JAQUEZ
It may be so,
Yet I had no command from him to see you.
My lord Alvarez, partner of his victory,
Charged me to find you and to tell you all 215
Lest you should grieve.

MARGARETTA
I thank him; 'twas most kind.
Oh! My Antonio! If I think thee false,
Forgive my weakness and remove my doubts.
Love grown to that excess I feel 220
Can scarce shake off the close attendant, jealousy.
Be gone, thou rude disturber of my peace;
My lord is true.

209. Not of me: Not think of me
211. Else I were: Or else I'd be
218. false: disloyal
222. thou rude disturber of my peace: jealousy
223. true: faithful

THE CONQUEST OF SPAIN

JAQUEZ
Of all discourse, Antonio is the theme,
For he's the very darling of the war, 225
Successful in the field as in his love.

MARGARETTA
By heaven, I wish him all he can desire:
Bright honor, boundless wealth, and full delight;
And, if there be a blessing yet superior,
Bestow it on the excellent Antonio. 230
What mean these rising tears! Why do I tremble!
Surely it bodes me ill; I'll not believe it.
'Tis poor Jacincta that distracts my mind,
And all my fears proceed from tender friendship.
Come, and I'll give the letters to my lord. 235
Alvarez has commended thy fidelity,
And on that score I know it was resolved
Thou shouldst be trusted and employed between us.
I hope thou art a faithful messenger.

JAQUEZ
Much rather let me die than be suspected. 240

MARGARETTA
Indeed thou art not, for I think thee honest;
Though, since hypocrisy is grown an art,
We scarce discern 'twixt falsehood and desert.

Exeunt

---

237. on that score: on that point, for that reason
243. desert: deserving

Act II, Scene iii

Enter CLOTHARIO

CLOTHARIO
Oh! Whither shall I fly to lose my fears? 1
The fair Jacincta is undone forever.
I saw her kneel, and weep, and beg in vain;
The angry king perceived my pitying looks
And with a frown commanded me away, 5
Dragging her himself along the floor.
Methinks I see the choleric general
Draw up his myrmidons against the palace.
But I have largely drank to drown these thoughts
And will be wise and sleep; who knows but things 10
May wear a better face when I awake.
I'm safe enough; none but the king can pass
While these are mine, the lady is secure.

Exit

---

7. choleric: angry
8. myrmidons: followers
13. these: keys

Act II, Scene iv

Enter JACINCTA

JACINCTA
Come back, thou tyrant! Barbarous ravisher! 1
And let me vent the fury of my soul.
Remorse, disease, ruin and infamy
Revenge my wrongs and haunt thee to thy grave.
Oh! I will range, like a mad bacchanal, 5
Through all the realms, proclaim my injuries,
And teach thy listening subjects to abhor thee.
Ungrateful king!
Is this the recompense thou givest my father
For all his painful years of blood and conquest? 10
And were his treacherous honors and his life
A train to ruin his unhappy daughter?
Oh! If I think, I shall grow impious,
And blame the authors of my wretched being.
Thou hopest, vain king, I should conceal my wrongs, 15
But I'll proclaim them both to heaven and earth;
I will pursue thee with incessant cries,
Waking and watchful as thy evil genius,
I'll seek new ways to terrify thy soul;
Pale, restless ghosts with me shall stalk their rounds 20
And help to break thy downy midnight slumbers.
Sleep shall forsake thy eyes, and peace thy mind:
Thou hast undone my virgin innocence.
Therefore no more of life: 'tis shame and torture.
But hear me, if thou wouldst preserve thy own, 25
Come back and kill me, so all's well again,
And my dear father still shall fight thy battles,
Unknowing of his hapless daughter's fate.
Oh, Julianus! The most wronged of men!

---

5. bacchanal: a follower of Bacchus, the god of wine
14. the authors of my wretched being: perhaps her parents or the gods
25. thy own: your own life
28. hapless: unlucky

How is thy loyal faith deluded now; 30
Whilst thou art winning trophies from Spain's enemies,
Spain has dishonored and imprisoned me.
Thou understandest not this, unless the winds
Upon their fleeting murmurs bear it to thee.
Oh! Gracious heaven, to whom shall I complain? 35
My father, Theomantius, Margaretta,
Living and dead to me are all alike;
What if the grave contain them, or the camp,
Or say they be imprisoned in a palace,
I have no aid, no comfort from their loves. 40
I cannot bear this load of infamy.
Oh, death! Thou gloomy path which most would shun,
Trembling I seek thee with unwearied steps,
And court thee to receive me in thy shade:
I'll search these hated rooms in hope to find thee. 45

Exit

30. deluded: made light of
37. all alike: all unable to help
38-39. What if the grave...a palace: Regardless of whether they are dead in a grave or alive in the palace
41. infamy: shame

Act II, Scene v

CLOTHARIO *sleeping, enter* JACINCTA

JACINCTA
All is barred: 1
Nothing left to assist my wild despair.
Ha! What wretch is this who ventures to sleep here?
Now, by my wrongs, the pander of the king.
And can he sleep, quiet, secure and fearless, 5
When I must never hope to rest again?
Oh! Ye impartial powers, is it just
That guilt should be at peace when virtue suffers?
What's here? His keys dropped from his drowsy hand:
Had I a murdering heart, these would instruct me, 10
And with his office, I could take his life.
But I have better thoughts: these set me free.
Welcome release! But whither shall I fly?
No matter where my wandering feet shall stray,
Alas! The wretched cannot lose their way. 15

Exit

End of Act II

---

3. ventures: dares
4. pander: pimp
11. with his office, I could take his life: Jacincta may imagine exposing Clothario's carelessness to get him executed.

Act III, Scene i

Scene: the camp

Enter DON GOMEZ, JULIANUS, ANTONIO, *and* ALVAREZ

JULIANUS
Thus far our prosperous arms drive back the invaders.   1
Antonio, worthy youth, let me embrace thee;
Much glory hast thou added to our name;
Thy early valor fires my aged heart;
Again my blood renews its sprightly round   5
When I reflect thy veins run full of it.

ANTONIO
Who would not lose the last dear ruddy drop
To merit praise from the mighty Julianus?
But I, of low desert, unknown to fame,
Must blush to be commended.   10

DON GOMEZ
Now by the watchful genius of loved Spain,
Throughout the warlike course of threescore years,
I swear I have not seen such forward virtue.
And to confirm thee, youth, my laboring thought
Does not alone produce the wind of praise,   15
In confirmation of my thoughts of him
I offer what to me of all the world
Is far most dear: my child, my only daughter.
The flattering court has called her fair; of that
Be you the judge; and this bold truth I promise: 20
Her weighty dowry shall exceed twice told
The richest maid's in Spain.

6. it: Julainus' family's blood
9. low desert: little deserving
14-15. to confirm thee...wind of praise: to prove my praise is not just words
19-20. of that / Be you the judge: you be the judge of her beauty

THE CONQUEST OF SPAIN

ANTONIO
Delia has every grace, is all perfection,
Beyond what my unpolished words can speak,
Yet the vast honor Antonio must decline, 25
Nor offer there a heart already filled
With the soft charms of a young, trusting innocence,
Whom to betray would stamp me for a villain,
Blast all my life to come with foul dishonor,
And soil the luster of my future actions. 30

DON GOMEZ
Again let me embrace thee, generous youth,
This freedom binds me yet more firmly thine;
Though not my son, my friend I'll ever call thee.

Trumpets sound

JULIANUS
Hark! We are summoned hence, the trumpets call,
And Spain's important busy hour draws nigh. 35
Remember, fellow soldiers, our great cause:
We for our mother fight, our native country.
What coward would not arm in such defense?
The invaders seem the cursed brood of hell,
Distinguished from the rest of humankind 40
By horrid black, the emblem of their souls.
Oh! Friends, can ye have patience to imagine
Your wives and daughters made a prey to these,
And not boil o'er with manly indignation?
Our women fear to look upon the monsters 45
Yet must become their slaves if we are vanquished:
Slaves to their pride and to their brutal pleasure.
Our gilded palaces and pleasant gardens
Will then been made a kennel for these dogs
Whilst we, with fruitless rage and idle grief, 50

32. freedom: openness
33. not my son: never to be my son-in-law
43. these: the Moors

Behold our temples sacked and rites profaned.
By heaven, I'm pleased, for sure, methinks I see
A cheerful eagerness in every face.
    (Trumpets sound again)
Come on, the charge is sounded, all's at stake.
Be valiant, and we'll drive these Africk fiends   55
Back to their scorching sun and desert sands.
    (Sound again)
Again! We come. Remember, fellow soldiers,
Religion, liberty, and deathless glory.

Exeunt all but ANTONIO *and* ALVAREZ

ANTONIO
Is not Jaquez yet returned from court?

ALVAREZ
Not yet. I wonder much at his delay.   60

ANTONIO
My friend,
To thee let me complain and own my weakness,
How my heart beats for the dear absent mourner:
Amidst the hurry of this warlike day,
Love will be heard, and Margaretta sighed for.   65
My soul is full of tenderness. If I fall,
As none is certain in the hour of battle,
I beg thee to regard my beauteous wife;
Defend her cause for thy Antonio's sake,
And let the dear unborn possess my fortunes.   70
Thou art a witness of our happy nuptials
And canst at leisure tell the general all.

---

58. deathless glory: glory that outlasts death
62. own: admit
67. none is certain: nothing is certain, no one is safe
69. her cause: her right to inherit from Antonio
70. the dear unborn: Margaretta's unborn child

ALVAREZ
Away with these ill omens.
Impartial fate will crown your matchless virtues;
Conquest, life, and love all wait your wishes, 75
Nor doubt my faith, for I'm wholly yours.

ANTONIO
'Tis well. Now to our troops, my Alvarez.
We'll not again embrace till flushed with victory.

Trumpets sound

ALVAREZ
These martial sounds fire my high-wrought blood
And animate my soul to death or glory. 80

ANTONIO
Oh! Love, be thou propitious to my prayer.
Be Margaretta safe, I nothing fear.

Exeunt

---

79. fire: bring fire to
81. propitious: favorable
82. Be Margaretta safe: As long as Margaretta is safe

Act III, Scene ii

Enter JAQUEZ

JAQUEZ
I think 'twas here, before the general's tent, 1
My lord commanded me to wait his coming.
In everything I have obeyed his orders:
Antonio's and bright Margaretta's letters
With care I have sunk deep in the swelling flood. 5
How this will aid my lord, I cannot guess,
But 'tis enough for me I have obeyed.

Enter ALVAREZ *with his sword drawn*

ALVAREZ
From the loud shouts of victory I fly
In search of the kind oracle of love.
My faithful Jaquez, welcome to my hopes. 10
Say, hast thou done as I directed thee,
And poisoned lovely Margaretta's soul?

JAQUEZ
I have, and left her pale with anxious thoughts,
And if in her letters she complained,
They're safe at bottom of the rapid stream 15
That parts the city and the camp.

ALVAREZ
Blessed news!
But now my artful engine we must haste.
The mighty balance is already turned:
A glorious conquest hovers on our side; 20

---

5. the swelling flood: the river
15. safe: safely hidden
18. engine: trickery, plot
20. A glorious conquest hovers on our side: Spain is set to beat the Moors

If I not see her ere Antonio reach her,
All my vain cobweb arts will be unraveled.
Stay near this place, and when Antonio sees thee,
For he with fond impatience seeks thee out,
Tell him his wife was busy with the ladies   25
And had not time to write but wished him safe.
Perhaps this may abate his fierce desires
And keep him here till I have gained my ends.

JAQUEZ
I shall be careful.

ALVAREZ
To redeem this stay   30
I'll to the battle, where the cowards fly
Like scattered leaves before the driving wind.
The general and his brave veteran bands
Are almost wearied with destroying. Hark!
  (Trumpets sound)
That seems the voice of an entire victory.   35
Away, be diligent, and wait my call.

Exeunt severally

---

21. If I not see her ere Antonio reach her: If I don't get to her before Antonio does
24. fond: silly
26. wished him safe: hoped he was safe
28. gained my ends: achieved my goal
30. To redeem this stay: To make up for my absence
34. wearied with destroying: exhausted by winning so thoroughly
35. entire: total, complete

Act III, Scene iii

Some MOORS *cross the stage as flying.*
Enter MULLYMUMEN *and several* OFFICERS

MULLYMUMEN
Descend thy sphere, thou burning deity,   1
Haste from our shame, go blushing to thy bed.
Thy sons we are, thou everlasting fire,
We who are stamped with thy own gloomy seal,
Which the whole ocean cannot wash away.   5
Shall these cold, ague cheeks, these smooth white skins,
Whom nature molds within her winter cave,
And with a palsy hand paints o'er for show,
Shall these make us recoil?

FIRST OFFICER
Did we for this leave our rich Africk shore?   10
With troops innumerable as our sands
Marched we unwearied o'er the barren earth,
Hungry and faint, yet with unbated courage,
To be at last destroyed like swarms of insects.

MULLYMUMEN
Where are we ranged from our defeated bands?   15

SECOND OFFICER
We seem to be among the general's tents,
Where we may view the luxury of Europe
And curse our shameful lot.

MULLYMUMEN
Ye partial powers!

---

1. burning deity: the sun
4. stamped with thy own gloomy seal: that is, darkened by the sun
6. these cold, ague cheeks, these smooth white skins: pale Spanish soldiers
15. Where are we ranged: Where have we come / Where are we

What have these gaudy things, this puny brood, 20
To do with war and fame?

Enter a MOOR

MOOR
Oh! Mighty prince,
If you would guard your life, fly hence with speed.
But for the heaps of slain that bar their way,
Ere this you had been lost. 25

MULLYMUMEN
Be dumb, thou coward,
Nor dare to whisper thy unmanly fears;
Turn from thy guilty flight and follow me:
Though now I cannot lead ye on to conquest,
I yet can show ye how to die. 30

FIRST OFFICER
Along, our hearts are ready for the sword.
'Tis glory that we fall with Mullymumen.

Exeunt

24. But for: If not for
26. dumb: silent
28. guilty flight: shameful retreat

Act III, Scene iv

Tunes of victory. Enter JULIANUS, DON GOMEZ, THEOMANTIUS, ALVAREZ, *and several* MOORS *as prisoners*

JULIANUS
Add to the cheerful shouts of victory 1
The pleasing news that Theomantius lives:
When your tired voices flag, that welcome sound
Will give new breath to your reviving joys.
My Theomantius lives; again, repeat it 5
Till rocks and streams catch the rebounding echo,
Till winds in gentle whispers greet Jacincta
With the glad tidings that her lover comes.
Think not, my noble warriors, you're neglected;
I swear you fought like the true sons of fame, 10
Like Spain's blessed guardians, bulwarks of your country.
But give me leave to ask this worthy youth
By what strange miracle he was preserved;
My soul longs to be feasted with the story.

THEOMANTIUS
Oh! 'Tis too much, I can't deserve this love, 15
But you are Jacincta's father, kind and good,
The generous source of every godlike virtue.

JULIANUS
No more of this, but say how you escaped
The fury of the Moors.

THEOMANTIUS
Sent by the king 20
With a bright train of eager, youthful warriors
To guard the coast and drive the invaders thence,

---

3. flag: tire

THE CONQUEST OF SPAIN

Not guessing half their power, we went too far
And soon appeared an easy destined prey,
A trifling handful to their numerous bands.   25
The old soldiers, of which we had not many,
Counseled a safe retreat but were not heard.
The fiery youth that rashly longed for action,
Who, fond of fame, were prodigal of life,
Rushed heedless on the foe: I blushing own   30
Myself the foremost in the mad attempt.
The subtle Moors gave our fierce courage way,
And saw us fledge our swords with many deaths,
Till, by the while, we were encompassed round,
Nor had we room to fight and fall like soldiers   35
But smothered by the press of barbarous slaves.
Myself was found among the Spanish youth,
Imagined dead,
But, lifted to the air, my vital breath returned.

JULIANUS
Blessed be the great auspicious power that saved thee;   40
I am all wonder.

THEOMANTIUS
Soon they confined me.
For what cause I was preserved, I knew not:
My wretched state denied all means of comfort,
No way was left to let you hear I lived,   45
Yet I bore all in hopes of this kind hour,
In hopes once more to fight by Julianus,
And once again to bless my longing eyes
With fair Jacincta's form. And heaven was gracious:

27. Counseled: Recommended
27. were not heard: were not heeded
29. prodigal: wasteful, reckless
30. own: acknowledge, admit
33. fledge: perhaps "feed" or "quench." Literally, of birds, to mature and become able to fly
42. they: the Moors

The day of battle came, and fears fell on them.   50
In their confusion, I was left unguarded;
I snatched the blessed occasion and escaped.
This sword I borrowed of a dying soldier,
To whom it was a useless burden grown;
With it I forced my way through the vile crowd   55
Who trembling fled from your victorious arm.
The rest you saw.

JULIANUS
I found thee by my side.
I thought it was thy genius fighting for me,
But trust me, youth, I have not felt more joy   60
Than when I grasped thee in my iron arms
And found it was indeed my Theomantius.

THEOMANTIUS
Oh! Happy change: my soul is full of bliss;
My country saved, and by my noble father;
Long have you given me leave to call you so,   65
And on that name eternal joys depend:
The nicer forms of awful love are past,
And my Jacincta now will glad my heart
With most sincere rejoicings for my safety.

JULIANUS
She will, my son, for she has wept thee truly,   70
Grown mad with grief, that scarce could my command
Keep her from desperation.

THEOMANTIUS
Oh! Lead me to her.

---

52. occasion: opportunity
53. of: from
59. genius: guardian angel
65. leave to call you so: permission to call you "father"
68. And: originally, "In"

THE CONQUEST OF SPAIN

Trumpets sound. Enter ANTONIO [*and* SOLDIERS], *with* MULLYMUMEN *and several* MOORISH OFFICERS *prisoner*

ANTONIO
Health to the general, and endless glory,
And may the foes of Spain be still like these, 75
Disarmed and bound, unable to destroy.
The war is at an end; fierce Mullymumen,
Who first urged this invasion, is your prisoner,
And waits your pleasure.

JULIANUS
'Tis well, my noble kinsman. 80
Thine was the act, and thine be the reward;
The king himself shall thank thee for this service.
But seest thou here, Antonio?

ANTONIO
Theomantius!

THEOMANTIUS
My dear Antonio! 85

They embrace

JULIANUS
Raise thy dejected eyes, thou haughty Moor.
Ill wert thou fitted for the doubtful field
If thou disdainest to bear the chance of war.
Be not dismayed, the king may spare thy life
And leave thee to repent thy rash ambition. 90
I'll not upbraid thee, since thou art in bonds,
But treat thee like a soldier.

---

75. still like these: always like these prisoners
88. bear the chance: take the risk, accept the outcome
91. upbraid: insult, abuse

MULLYMUMEN
I would thank you,
But hatred and despair restrain my tongue.
When first I landed on the Spanish coast, 95
A thirst of glory urged me to the war;
This cursed defeat has made me hate your country.
The legions I have lost I would revenge:
With burning envy I behold thy virtue.
Even our complexions are more near allied 100
Than are our souls.

JULIANUS
No matter, surly prince.
        [*to* SOLDIERS]
Here, guard them well, yet be your usage gentle;
Teach them the difference of our Christian world,
And force them to forget their brutal tempers. 105

Exeunt the MOORS, *guarded* [*by* SOLDIERS]

Enter a SOLDIER

SOLDIER
My lord, a messenger from court desires admittance.

JULIANUS
Quick let him enter.

Exit SOLDIER

Enter LODOVICUS

LODOVICUS
The king, great Julianus, greets you well.
His waiting scouts have given him an account

100. more near allied: more similar (that is, not at all)
105. tempers: perhaps "moods," or perhaps "natures"

Of the success of this victorious day. 110
He thanks the soldiers for their loyal courage,
And his large donatives shall well reward them,
Besides the plunder of the Africk tents,
Which he most freely gives them.

JULIANUS
Sent he thee 115
With needless orders to direct the soldiers?
The king shall be obeyed, it is my duty,
But sure he'll leave the discipline to me.

LODOVICUS
Then, 'tis the will of potent Rhoderique
That you decamp not far from hence, my lord, 120
No nearer to the city, as you're loyal,
Nor once approach the court till his commands
Have given you license.

JULIANUS
I think we shall not, sir.
Go bear this message to my royal master: 125
I'll not dispute his pleasure but obey.

LODOVICUS
Next—

THEOMANTIUS
Have you more orders?

LODOVICUS
Next, he requires the prisoners they be sent him;
The castle there is stronger to secure them. 130

112. donatives: donations
113. Besides: In addition to
121. as you're loyal: if you are loyal
123. license: permission
129. sent him: sent to him

JULIANUS
The king shall have them with convenient speed.
But prithee, do thou leave us; 'tis most strange:
There's something in thee which offends.

LODOVICUS
Farewell.

Exit bowing

JULIANUS
My prisoners! And not presented by my hand!　　　135
What! Not the poor returns of thanks and praise
For all my age has done! 'Tis very hard.
'Tis my great master's will, and I submit.
Ha! What didst thou forget! Unkind old man!
How couldst thou so neglect thy only comfort?　　　140
I asked not of my dear Jacincta's health,
The gentle maid.

THEOMANTIUS
Forgive my fears;
Is my adored Jacincta then at court?

JULIANUS
I left her there.　　　145

THEOMANTIUS
Alas!

JULIANUS
Why sighs my son?

THEOMANTIUS
I know not. Sorrow often comes uncalled.

135-137. My prisoners!...'Tis very hard: Julianus laments that he will not have the honor of personally presenting his prisoners to the king.

ANTONIO
The general looks sad; let us revive him.
  [*to* JULIANUS]
My lord, I cannot bear to see you thus. 150
Disperse the cloud that hangs upon your brow,
Nor let the king disturb your sacred peace.
Your virtues cannot lose by his ingratitude;
Not in Spain's ancient annals can we find
A chief like you, renowned for noble acts: 155
Famed Julianus, ever blessed with conquest,
The soul of war and darling of the soldiers;
For you they'd sacrifice their lives with pleasure,
So would we all.

TOGETHER
All. 160

JULIANUS
Away; you are to blame.
Direct the soldiers to obey the king.
It is their duty, nor do I want their service.
I pray you all retire, I would be private.
Refresh yourselves, and glad the wearied army; 165
They want you.

THEOMANTIUS
How can we consent to go
And leave our noble general in sadness?

ANTONIO
Rather let us disobey.

JULIANUS
I entreat you, 170

---

153. lose: decrease
157. darling: beloved one
161. you are to blame: you are in the wrong (for siding with Julianus over the king)

I have business in my tent, I'd write to the king.

THEOMANTIUS
All peace and happiness be ever yours.

Exeunt all but JULIANUS

JULIANUS
Confine me from the court, send for my prisoners:
Are these the honors I've thus hardly won?
Are these the wreaths with which he decks my brows? 175
How will my faithful soldiers bear the wrongs?
But I'm hushed, for where's my boasted loyalty
If with my murmurings I upbraid the king?
Perhaps he means me favor in this business,
And to appear at court so soon after this action 180
Might, by the crowd, be thought too popular.
He is most wise, and I condemn myself,
For he has given me safety in this banishment;
Again, my prisoners may be safest there.
Begone, repining thoughts. 185

Enter a SOLDIER

SOLDIER
My lord,
A Moorish lady, who has suffered wrong,
Presses to your presence.

JULIANUS
Haste and admit her.
    (*Exit* SOLDIER)
I have a daughter of that lovely form; 190
Remembering her, more dear to me than life,

---

174. thus hardly won: won with this much hardship
181. too popular: showing off
185. repining: discontented

Even all her injured sex claim my protection.
And when I have told my conquest to the king,
My child, my poor Jacincta, then shall know
That, for her sake, I did a pious act. 195
(*Enter* JACINCTA *disguised in a Moorish habit,*
veiled and weeping. [JACINCTA *kneels*])
Thy mournful look calls up compassion in me;
Thou seemest a statue meant to express despair.
Why kneelest thou? Art thou wronged?
Name me the hated author,
And, though he be my kinsman or my friend, 200
Death shall divide him from us and revenge thee.

JACINCTA
Oh! My dear father!

JULIANUS
Thy father? Who has wronged him?

JACINCTA
A great commander.

JULIANUS
Under me? 205

JACINCTA
Above you.

JULIANUS
Who's above a general?
None but the king, the mighty Rhoderique;
He would not wrong thy father.

JACINCTA.
What was Tarquin? 210

192. all her injured sex: all women
199. author: (of your despair)
200. though he be: even if he is
210. Tarquin: a Roman king's son, the rapist of Lucrece

JULIANUS
An imperial ravisher.

JACINCTA
Such an one
Was in those days a monster.

JULIANUS
Prithee be plain.

JACINCTA
Have not you, sir, a daughter?

JULIANUS
If I have not 215
I am the wretchedest man that this day lives,
For all the wealth I have is hoarded in her.

JACINCTA
Then hear my woes for that loved daughter's sake.

JULIANUS
Rise and speak them.

JACINCTA
No, let me kneel still; 220
Such a resemblance of a daughter's duty
Will make you mindful of a father's love.

JULIANUS (*weeping*)
Trust me, it shall.
So nearly does thy voice resemble hers,
That see, already I have caught thy grief. 225

---

221. Such a resemblance of a daughter's duty: My kneeling resemblance of a dutiful daughter

JACINCTA
Then call your utmost reason to your aid,
Arm you with noble patience, and regard me.
Say your daughter
By some cursed hand was dragged to violation,
Think if you see her torn from her apartment,   230
Her loosened hair wound round the villain's hand,
Calling in vain on heaven and her father,
Her tender bosom bruised, her garments rent
With struggling to escape the foul dishonor;
Think if you saw her kneeling on the earth,   235
Imploring pity of those cruel monsters,
More savage than the beasts that hunt in forests,
Think that you saw them bear her through the palace,
Deaf to her prayers, her tears, her threats and cries,
And yielded her up a prey to raging lust,   240
How would you bear this scene, or how revenge it?

JULIANUS
Oh! 'Tis too hard a question to resolve
Without a solemn counsel held within,
Where justice, honor and paternal love
Must weigh this wrong and guide my erring rage.245

JACINCTA
Say this was done by him you most revere.

JULIANUS
Thou shakest my soul as it were so indeed
And not a figure artfully designed
To alarm my thoughts and move my aching heart
To a more tender sense of thy misfortunes.   250
What canst thou mean?

---

233. rent: torn
236. of: from
247. as it were so: as if it were so

JACINCTA (*throwing up her veil*)
See here the injured, ravished, lost Jacincta.
The blotted relict of a ruined maid;
Pity my shame, and spare my faltering tongue
The hated repetition of my wrongs. 255

JULIANUS
Horror, amazement, and distraction seize me,
My brain turns round, and my full eyes run o'er:
Oh! Quick, prevent a traitorous suspicion,
Destroy the embryo ere it grow too powerful,
And name that enemy to the king and me. 260
Why dost thou pause?

JACINCTA
In pity to your age,
That yet a moment you may calm your grief
With thinking o'er the glories of your life:
Your constant valor and unshaken loyalty, 265
The numerous trophies of your active youth,
And this last triumph of your hoary age:
For when you have heard who 'tis has done this deed,
You will repent the honors you have won,
And wish unacted all your toils of war 270
Thus cruelly rewarded.

JULIANUS
'Tis too much,
I cannot bear this torturing suspense;
Name me the villain and remove my doubts.

JACINCTA
The ungrateful king; 'tis he has wrought this ruin. 275

253. relict: remains, leftover
258. a traitorous suspicion: Julianus suspects the king but rejects that thought as traitorous
259. embryo: seed of doubt
271. Thus cruelly rewarded: That have been thus cruelly rewarded

THE CONQUEST OF SPAIN

The king, for whom so often you have conquered,
Has all your faithful services repaid
With brutal wrongs, eternal infamy, and never-ceasing woe.

JULIANUS
Oh! Gnawing anguish!
Saidst thou the king? Then all revenge is lost,   280
And we must bear our heavy load of shame.
Tamely as cowards I must bear this wrong,
Nor once attempt to wash thy stains in blood.

JACINCTA
Oh! Let the grave receive me
From the sad eyes of an indulgent father,   285
Whose heart bleeds for my sufferings.

JULIANUS
Rise, Jacincta,
And let me pour my soul in fondness o'er thee;
Down, ye tumultuous thoughts that rack my brain.
It is the king: let that control your fury.   290
Alas! My child, I had almost forgot;
Thy Theomantius lives.

JACINCTA
Malicious stars!
He lives but to augment my sufferings;
Had he been dead, he had not known my shame.   295
What though he lives, he can never be mine:
No more my eyes with pleasure must behold him.
From all the joys of life and virtuous love,
From all the comfort which glad nature yields,
The king, the cruel king has cut me off.   300
Hatred and rage have now possessed my thoughts,
And all to come is horror and despair.

283. wash thy stains: avenge thy shame
293. stars: fate
296. What: So what

JULIANUS
Oh! Had I listened to thy juster fears,
All had been well;
Into my inner tent retire a while   305
Till I shall call thee forth.

JACINCTA
Let me go
From whence I never may again return.
Where shall I find a place to shroud my shame?
To rocks, to barren deserts let me fly,   310
To dusky caverns, far from human sight,
To solitary groves whose untrod paths
Are dark and silent as are those below,
Where gloomy poplar and the baneful yew
Compose a dismal shade, fitting my woes: 315
Where bats and owls build their aboding nests,
And adders crawl on the unwholesome ground:
There undisturbed let me indulge my grief
Till death appears and brings me wished relief.

Exit

JULIANUS
Now let me think, though thought be worse than hell;   320
Suppose I shut this darling rifled made
Within a living tomb, some pious cloister,
And bury my great master's fault in silence,
So he perhaps may boast him of my injuries
And glory in the tame old man's destruction;   325
So, he might give loose to lawless power:
Nor wives, nor daughters, be they young and fair,
Can then escape his vicious appetite.

314. poplar: a pale white tree
314. yew: a bush with poisonous berries
321. rifled: stolen
322. a living tomb, some pious cloister: e.g., a nunnery
327. Nor wives: Neither wives

No, I'll proclaim his barbarous violence,
Yet still preserve his person and the throne; 330
Amidst his parasites I'll force my way,
Set all his numerous crimes before his eyes
And make him loathe the vices he has acted.
Who waits there? Let the commanders enter.
    (*Enter* THEOMANTIUS, ANTONIO, DON GOMEZ,
    ALVAREZ, *and* ATTENDANTS.)
Which of you all in this mistaken crowd 335
Hailed Julianus happy? Oh my friends!
There stands upon this narrow space of earth
A wretch more cursed, more pressed with misery
Than ever yet your pitying eyes beheld.

THEOMANTIUS
Then fate must be unjust and Spain ungrateful; 340
Through all the various turns of busy life,
Still have you trod the unerring path of virtue.

ANTONIO
In war the great protector of your country,
In peace the blessed example of all good:
How can you be unhappy? 345

ALVAREZ
Oh, ease our hearts,
And let us know from whence this grief proceeds.

ANTONIO
A swift redress shall banish all your cares,
And joy shall be restored.

DON GOMEZ
If from the king 350

---

330. preserve: defend
331. parasites: cronies
336. Hailed: Called

You have received a base indignity,
As by his messages we faintly guess,
Know, all the forces are at your command.
The nation you've redeemed is wholly yours.

THEOMANTIUS
And reason must be taught luxurious Rhoderique   355
If he betrays he wants it.

ANTONIO
With our lives
We will defend our glorious general.
Tyranny shall not reach him.

JULIANUS
Nephew, hold.   360
That guilty voice offends that leads to treason.
Saidst thou I should not suffer tyranny?
Alas, alas, who can secure the wretched?
It is not in the power of gracious heaven
To heal my sorrows. Oh, perfidious king!   365

THEOMANTIUS
Still keep your prisoners spite of his command.

JULIANUS
Oh! Were that all, how calmly could I bear,
How easily resign this high command,
My sooty prisoners and these useless trophies;
Had all the malice of inveterate stars   370
Been only wrecked on my devoted head,
Had I alone sustained this shock of fate,

---

351. base indignity: vile insult
355. taught: taught to
356. betrays: reveals
356. wants: lacks
363. secure: save
365. perfidious: treacherous

Without a murmur I had borne the load;
Had Rhoderique pursued me as an enemy,
Confined me to a horrid loathsome prison, 375
And galled me with vile ignominious chains,
Yet I had borne it all with constant patience,
Sat down beneath his wrath and blessed the tyrant.
But he has found a way to wound my soul
That from my aged eyes draws floods of tears, 380
And from my tongue extorts unwilling curses;
I had but one weak part: a beauteous woman,
To whom nature has been lavish of her graces
And heaven given bright, untainted honor,
Which in her father's absence— 385

THEOMANTIUS
Ye sacred powers!
Guard my Jacincta's virtue.

JULIANUS
No power would.
    (*Exit, and re-enter with* JACINCTA)
Here, fellow soldiers, view this fair undone,
This mourning shadow of departed fame, 390
This bosom treasure of a poor old man,
Abused and blotted with foul stains of lust
By the ungrateful king, in whose long service
I am grown ancient, withered and decayed.
Behold her thus disguised to find her father. 395

THEOMANTIUS
Jacincta!
Are these the soft delights I hoped at meeting?
Would I had died indeed among the Moors.

373. had: would have
376. galled: chafed
383. of: in
397. hoped at meeting: hoped to find
398. Would I had: I wish I had

JACINCTA
Shame and confusion choke my rising words,
And woes like mine are not to be expressed. 400
Oh! Theomantius, turn away thy eyes
From viewing my dishonor.

THEOMANTIUS
Fair suffering saint,
Forbid me not to gaze upon thy beauties.
They and thy noble mind are still the same, 405
Sublime and chaste, unsullied by the tyrant,
That robber, that cursed bane to all my joys.

ANTONIO
What now, alas, is Margaretta's fate?

ALVAREZ
Perhaps the same.

ANTONIO
Stop thy ill-boding words, 410
And let us hasten and prevent the tyrant.

ALVAREZ (*aside*)
I lose my aim, or I am there before you.
   [*aloud*]
You have forgot we are forbid the court.

THEOMANTIUS
What is it guards our arms from just revenge?
Come on, and let us rush upon the tyrant, 415
Tear him from his voluptuous seat of power
And show the monster bare, the beast of rapine.

ANTONIO
The curse of Spain and burden of the throne.

---

412. lose my aim: miss my mark, lose my goal
417. rapine: seizure, rape

THE CONQUEST OF SPAIN

THEOMANTIUS
Oh loved Jacincta, thou art still my wife;
As such, I will revenge thy barbarous wrongs. 420
Thy godlike father made thee mine by promise,
And with the ravisher's blood I'll wash thy stains,
Then take thee to my arms.

JACINCTA
Forbear, forbear,
Nor ever let such sounds approach my ears. 425
Judge not so poorly of the lost Jacincta
To think I'll bring pollution to thy bed;
With sadness and the grave I have made a contract,
And with my life alone my griefs must end.

DON GOMEZ
Why seems our mighty general lost in thought, 430
Since here are ready hearts and hands to serve you?

THEOMANTIUS
Let us set free the prisoners of war
And join with them against the adulterous king;
He has abused the royal dignity
And must resign the gilded reins of empire 435
To one more worthy.

JULIANUS
Hold that impious breath!
What unseen ills has headlong rage brought on me,
When vilest treason to my face is uttered!
Though Rhoderique has acted most ignobly, 440
Yet still he is a king, and we his subjects.
I urged my wrongs, and meant that he should know it,
By fear and shame to bring him to remorse,

---

419. wife: fiancee
427. bring pollution to thy bed: that is, by marrying him
442. urged: pleaded (in a letter)

And guard his royal soul from future crimes;
If I should fail in this, which heaven forbid, 445
I dare not lift my sword against my sovereign;
Much less should any here; you are not injured.
Mine is the wrong, and I must learn to bear it
While you retain your duty to your king.

THEOMANTIUS
I have no duty now, nor no allegiance; 450
My ruined love calls loud for speedy vengeance.
All that revere the glorious general
And would not see his honor trampled on,
All that are touched with chaste Jacincta's wrongs,
Follow me, and to the listening soldiers 455
Let's speak our resolutions.

ANTONIO
Thus with drawn swords we'll seek the ravisher,
While trembling guilt, the source of cowardice,
Shall yield him to his fate.

JULIANUS
Where are my troops? 460
Have I no power left to stay this outrage?
My faithful soldiers, they will yet obey me
And guard these thoughtless traitors from perdition.

THEOMANTIUS
Not one will stir but to revenge their general;
Let them look on that lovely ruined temple 465
Where innocence and virtue sat enshrined,
Then bid a whirlwind stop its giddy course,
Or bid the sea restrain its flowing tide,
For these your voice much sooner might command

447. injured: insulted
460. Where are my troops?: rhetorical; the troops defy him
463. perdition: damnation (for treason)
465. ruined temple: Jacincta

THE CONQUEST OF SPAIN

Than the fierce rage of your offended soldiers.   470

JULIANUS
Ha, by my honor, which abhors this treason,
My own arm shall execute what they refuse;
Now let me find but one audacious rebel
That dares oppose my will and aid this madness;
I swear that man whose weapon's left unsheathed,   475
My sword shall find a passage to his heart.

JACINCTA [*coming between them*]
Oh, hold, my father! Oh, my friends, forbear.
Or rushing thus between the lifted points,
Let sad Jacincta find a fate most welcome.

THEOMANTIUS
Lovely sufferer, 'tis thy matchless charms   480
That fire thy Theomantius to revenge.
Come on, my lords, let's leave the general,
And show our cause was just by our success.

Exeunt all but JULIANUS *and* JACINCTA

JULIANUS
Why thus untimely didst thou bar my fury?
Oh, my child, thou period to my fame,   485
Thy fate has every way undone thy father.

JACINCTA [*kneeling*]
Then sheath your sword in this unhappy breast,
But do not look thus cruelly upon me;
Behold me prostrate, crawling on the earth;
All that my lifted eyes and hands implore,   490

---

472. they: my soldiers
481. fire: spur
484. bar: block
485. period: end

All that I hope and wish is only death;
When I am mouldered into native dust,
All will again be well, the king be safe,
My wrongs no more shall wake the sleeping vengeance,
Rebellion shall be still as my complaints; 495
Bury the hateful story in oblivion,
And peace and glory will again revive.

JULIANUS
Rise, wretched woman. No, thou hast much to do
Before the peaceful grave receives thy sorrows.
Thy gentle power may yet prevent this storm. 500
Thy Theomantius loves; then quick pursue him,
Calm his wild rage, and I'll restrain the rest.
Ye powers, why was long life miscalled a blessing?
Why from a train of glorious ancestors
Was that rich jewel, fame, committed to me? 505
Why did I husband and improve the stock
Even to the highest pitch of dazzling glory?
Unwearied with my toils, in youthful spring,
In full blown summer and in ripened autumn,
Still the full vintage came and crowned my wishes; 510
Not grizzled winter checked the warm pursuit;
But oh, how vainly does the hero boast
That honor which so many dangers cost,
So many years, thus in one moment lost.

Exeunt

End of Act III

---

495. still: as still, as quiet
506. husband: cultivate
506. the stock: (of fame)
508-509. spring...summer...autumn: the seasons of life
512. vainly: pointlessly

Act IV, Scene i

[*Scene: inside the castle*]

Enter MARGARETTA

MARGARETTA
Oh, jealousy! Busy, tormenting fiend,   1
Where didst thou lurk? Where was thy dark abode
Before thou entredst here to wreck my peace?
Sure in some place where only horrors dwell,
Where furies howl and pointed scorpions sting,   5
Where anxious thoughts forever banish sleep,
And false suspicions still are murmuring round,
Where after death the guilty are confined:
Oh, no, for there is everlasting hate,
And thou canst only be where love exists,   10
For thou indeed art love, but love diseased,
Madness and restless pain to all that know thee.
No word, no friend come yet from my Antonio
To give my laboring mind a dawn of ease.
What's poor Jacincta's fate, I cannot guess;   15
Thus shut from human view I nothing know.

Enter ALVAREZ

ALVAREZ
Hail, beauteous Margaretta.

MARGARETTA
Alvarez here,
Then my sad eyes again behold a friend.
What news from war, is my Antonio safe?   20

---

4. Sure: Surely
5. furies: fearsome women, vengeful spirits
8. Where after death the guilty are confined: hell
9. there: in hell

ALVAREZ
The Moors have yielded to our conquering arms.

MARGARETTA
Unkind, why tell'st thou me of foes subdued?
Blasted be all your laurels, all your triumphs,
If my loved hero lives not to partake them.

ALVAREZ
He lives in perfect health and boundless joy, 25
The foremost palm was his.

MARGARETTA
Now blessings on thee,
New life thou bring'st me and new kindling pleasures;
But now, and I was shaded with despair;
Thou hast dispersed the cloud and cheered my heart. 30
Ha, I minded not thy sad dejected posture,
Thy folded arms, thy eyes bent to the earth,
As if they sullenly forbid my transport.
Oh, Alvarez, forbear to give me fears.
Enough of grief I have already felt; 35
Compel not the return of torturing doubt.

ALVAREZ
Command thyself, thou loveliest of thy sex,
With mercy to forgive.

MARGARETTA
Forgive what, whom?
'Tis as I feared. Be still, my boding thoughts; 40
Why do you whisper ruin to my love
And by these hopeless pangs forestall despair?

23. laurels: wreathes of honor
26. palm: a symbol of victory
29. But now: Just now
31. minded not: didn't notice
33. transport: gladness

Why do I shake before I hear my fate?
Oh, give me ease, and quickly tell me who
The wretched Margaretta must forgive? 45

ALVAREZ
Forgive your husband, who implores your pity,
And swears by all the ills he has endured,
The loathed constraint his destiny imposed,
The flame your eyes first lighted in his breast
Still lives and burns with unabated force 50
And reigns the tyrant of his days.

MARGARETTA
Yet go on,
Though at each accent nature fast decays,
And all the props of feeble life are sinking.

ALVAREZ
The general, whose will none dares dispute, 55
Much less Antonio, his peculiar charge,
Great Julianus swear that it should be,
And he with grief unwillingly obeyed,
With secret anguish and with stifled shame,
Against his soul he espoused the beauteous Delia, 60
Nor durst refuse and plead his former vows.

MARGARETTA
'Tis finished.

She faints. [ALVAREZ holds her]

ALVAREZ
Oh, yield not to despair.

---

56. his peculiar charge: for whom he especially cares
58. he: Antonio
60. espoused: married
61. plead his former vows: refuse by way of his previous (secret) marriage

[*aside*]
By heaven, 'tis joy, 'tis ecstasy of bliss
To hold her in my arms, though cold and dying.　　65
My eager fires have warmed her back to life.

MARGARETTA [*reviving*]
Stand off, and give my boundless sorrows way,
If I should tear these robes, this hair, this breast,
Could Alvarez condemn my just distraction?
Oh, is it possible to bear this wound?　　70
Antonio false? Then virtue is no more.
He that has flattered, and outsworn his sex
As far as ever they did sacred truth,
Witness, ye louring, inauspicious stars,
That with unlucky beams beheld our nuptials,　　75
And you superior planets, sun, and moon,
All, all have heard his vows and seen him false.

ALVAREZ
Yet I have more to say.

MARGARETTA
The rest is needless.
What canst thou tell me beyond misery?　　80
Am I not cursed, is not my portion full?
What then remains but to despair and die?
Let me indulge that thought: I like it well.
Death is the gentle remedy of grief.
That only path is open to my view　　85
That can conduct me to eternal rest.

ALVAREZ
The bridegroom mourns and bends his pensive head,
Nor can he force one smiled to grace his nuptials,

---

69. distraction: extreme grief
72. outsworn his sex: sworn more than any man
74. louring: frowning

His sighs and watery eyes too plain betray
The inward anguish of his bleeding love; 90
With conscious blushes he implored my aid,
And, as his long-tried friend, urged me to see you
And soften this relation ere he came.
He owns his crime, though much compelled to act it,
And durst not write till you resolve to pardon. 95
He invokes the soft befriending powers of love
And all the fierce disposers of revenge,
To punish, as they ought, his horrid perjuries
If still he loves you not as dear as ever.
He holds you still the darling of his soul 100
And begs you'll condescend to share his fortunes.

MARGARETTA
Can he believe I will, on such base terms?
Am I not born even noble as himself?
And dares he offer me his odious pensions?
To what obscure retreat art thou to guide me, 105
Where, to conceal his crime and my disgrace,
This wretched burden of my teeming womb,
This unborn babe, may be in stealth brought up
By a vile name to my great race unknown?
Oh, I shall rave! 'Tis not to be supported: 110
All that is soft and gentle in my nature,
This most unequaled wrong has quite destroyed.
Warm with rage, I'll seek this unjust rival,
And through a thousand wounds let forth her guilt,
And glut my soul with vengeance. 115

ALVAREZ
Fruitless design,

---

93. this relation: (the news of) this relationship
94. owns: acknowledges
101. fortunes: money, luck, or future
102. base: vile
109. a vile name: bastard
116. Fruitless design: Pointless plan

Is she not compassed round with faithful friends?
Nay, think: should you proclaim your injuries,
And he disowns the charge, who would believe?
Who would you bring to listen to the story   120
And judge it other than the effects of frenzy?
Few favor helpless innocence.

MARGARETTA
Most true.
    (*aside*)
Oh ready mischief, thou art quick of thought.
My beating heart begins to calm apace.   125
I am a woman, a much injured woman,
But I will learn to bear my load of woe.
    [*aloud*]
Shall I not see him more, is that denied?

ALVAREZ (*aside*)
'Tis what I wished to hear! Now, Venus aid me!
    [*aloud*]
It was his own request that you would see him: 130
The important blessing which he bade me sue for.
Stern Julianus has most rashly sworn
Sure death to all who this night leave the camp,
Yet your Antonio will not fear to come;
He'll steal through dreadfullest shades to those loved arms.
Soon as 'tis dark, expect him here.

MARGARETTA
'Tis well.
Which way gained you admittance to this place?

---

118. should you: if you
119. disowns: denies
122. innocence: or possibly "innocents"
124. Oh ready mischief...: This is marked as an aside in the 1705, but Margaretta is still speaking of Antonio as she does not suspect Alvarez. She probably begins speaking aloud again at line 128.
129. Venus: goddess of love
131. sue: plead

[ALVAREZ]
The governor Lothario is my friend.
By his unquestioned power, since you permit, 140
Antonio too may pass, but in disguise,
For if he speaks, or if a look be known,
'Tis certain fate, the general is fixed.

[MARGARETTA]
Behind this lodging there is a dark alcove,
And thither I'll convey him, hold my heart: 145
Perhaps I yet may bring him back to virtue,
For marrying twice, my lord, to me appears
With all the horrors of presumption, sin.
Sure 'tis afronting heaven, whose sacred fears
Are thus profaned to aid their vile designs. 150

ALVAREZ
Now you think calmly.

MARGARETTA
Oh, I have considered.
Passion is madness, and I am well at peace.
What hour will lord Antonio design to come
And bless his widowed slave? 155

ALVAREZ
At ten exactly.

MARGARETTA
Here he shall find me, ready to receive him;
And ere the ruddy streaks of day appear,

---

139. Lothario: perhaps a misspelling of "Clothario," whom the king calls the "keeper of this tower" (II.i.68). Alternatively, a different character whose name means "seducer" or "libertine" after a character by Miguel de Cervantes.
143. fixed: determined
149. sacred fears: unclear meaning
153. and I am: originally, "and am"

Oh, Alvarez, thou shalt confess my power
And own no doting, no deluded woman, 160
Ere parted with the charming man she loved,
The dearest only object of her wishes,
With half that ease as I. No more; good night.

ALVAREZ
Good night, and may you be forever blessed.

Exit MARGARETTA

ALVAREZ
Jaquez, come forward. 165

Enter JAQUEZ

JAQUEZ
Have you succeeded?

ALVAREZ
Beyond my hopes. Invention, now I thank thee;
There was no other way but this to gain her.
Had I not wound her up to jealousy,
Her lofty, piercing sense, quick at inquiry, 170
Had found me out and baffled my attempt;
Now, she herself conducts me to my bliss.
Oh love, be kind, and give me once possession,
The consequence I leave to hell or fate.

JAQUEZ
This busy night will favor thefts of love; 175
None are at leisure to observe the amorous.
Both court and camp are all in loud confusion.
The king by Theomantius is proclaimed

160. And own: And acknowledge (that)
170. sense: mind
171. Had: Would have
173. give me: (if you) give me

A tyrant and a brutal ravisher;
The crowd, as ever wont, embrace rebellion 180
And vow revenge; the general raves in vain.

ALVAREZ
No matter, let destruction rage and reign;
Even in the midst of ruin, I'll possess.
And if it must be so, then perish pleased.

JAQUEZ [*pointing*]
See, the king and court. 185

ALVAREZ
Let us avoid them.
And do thou haste and get me some disguise.
Oh, lovely Margaretta, bless my hopes,
Kindly receive them, and forgive the villain
Thy eyes have made: till I their beauties saw, 190
I never swerved from honor's rigid law.

Exeunt

---

180. as ever wont: as is ever their way
184. it must be so: (that I'm to die)
189. Receive them, and forgive: originally, "receive, then and forgive"

Act IV, Scene ii

Enter KING, CLOTHARIO, and GUARDS

KING
Hopest thou to live, unthinking lump of negligence,   1
That durst be careless of the charge I gave?
Couldst thou not guard a woman from escape?
A man had looked thy coward soul to fear;
Jacincta had not courage to outbrave thee,   5
That angelorm.

CLOTHARIO
If your majesty–

KING
Forbear thy vile excuse, nothing shall save thee.
Brings not her flight inevitable ruin?
By this the haughty general rages high,   10
And well I know to expect the black event.
Had the wronged fair remained within our power,
I might have found some soft auspicious moments
To have soothed her injuries and fixed my joys.
But thou, ill-fated wretch, hast blasted all.   15

Enter LODOVICUS

LODOVICUS
Oh royal sir!

KING
Why is thy pale disorder!
Express thyself as it becomes a man.

---

2. charge: an order, but also, someone who is left in another's care
6. angelorm: unknown meaning; perhaps a misspelling of "angel form"
10. By this: By now

LODOVICUS
Theomantius is revolted.

KING
Thou dreamest; he's dead. 20

LODOVICUS
He lives, and heads the vanquished Moors against you,
And brings them on even to your palace gates;
Aloud he does proclaim Jacincta's rape,
And by his manly rage and moving grief,
He augments the fury of the kindling soldiers: 25
The storm's at hand.

KING
Living, and joined the Moors!
Then shame and sure destruction comes apace.
And Julianus, he foments the uproar,
And stands the foremost in this cursed rebellion, 30
Old venerable traitor.

LODOVICUS
You wrong him much.
Though injured most, he only scorns the name.
O'erwhelmed with grief, he runs amidst the crowd,
Commands, exhorts, conjures, but all in vain: 35
Tears off his hoary hair, and sues with tears;
His wondrous virtue moves the sons of war,
But, against his will, he moves them to revenge.

KING
By heaven the slave is eloquent on ruin.
Well, if my setting hour be fixed above, 40

---

20. Thou dreamest; he's dead: originally, "Thou dream'st his dead"
25. augments: increases
28. apace: quickly
40. fixed above: decided by heaven

In vain I struggle for a longer date:
Why are we flattered with a mimic sway,
Why made to think whole armies wait our nod?
In them our strength and not our safety lies.
This glaring ill sets my past faults in view, 45
But I'll disdain to own I've done amiss.
Resolved, I'll be myself, and brave my fate.

CLOTHARIO
Would I had courage, too; we all shall want it.

KING
Guard well the avenues that lead to the castle;
Myself will sally forth and face this tempest. 50
The moon is rising and will guide my arms.
Who knows what fortune may attend my steps?
The face of majesty may awe the slaves,
And teach those daring wretches, born our subjects,
To know their duty, and return to mercy, 55
And force the conquered Moors to reassume
The slavery this morning sun imposed.
All that have hearts, follow me.

CLOTHARIO
'Twas your command that I should guard the castle.

KING
See that thou dost it well. Thy fate's deferred. 60
Come on, your king commands, and country pleads,
Spain is no more the hour that Rhoderique bleeds.

Exeunt

42. mimic sway: phony command
46. done amiss: done (anything) wrong
48. Would: I wish
48. want: need
53. slaves: rebels
62. Spain... bleeds: Spain is lost if Rhoderique bleeds

Act IV, Scene iii

Enter ALVAREZ *disguised*

ALVAREZ
'Tis dark as my own thoughts. This is the hour,   1
And this the place where Margaretta meets me.
Oh, expectation, thou uneasy blessing,
Thou fuel to desire, thou restless doubt,
Thou painful rack to every eager wish,   5
Thou heavenly prospect in the dawn of love.
Ha! What noise is that? Be still, my heart,
Nor swell, nor beat before thy time.

Enter MARGARETTA

MARGARETTA [*aside*]
He's come.
I hear the traitor's voice in distant accents.   10
        [*aloud*]
So soon arrived, Antonio.

ALVAREZ
Softly, the same.

MARGARETTA
Lend me your hand that I may lead you in.

ALVAREZ
'Tis here, my life.

MARGARETTA
Oh! You are strangely welcome.   15
We'll find a lone recess shall well express it.

Leads him in

---

15. strangely: very
16. shall: that shall

Act IV, Scene iv

Re-enter MARGARETTA *with a light and dagger*

MARGARETTA
Already he's disarmed and laid to rest!   1
Now for my purpose, to perform a deed
Which but to think, some fleeting hours since,
Had turned me to a statue. Wondrous change!
This taper when the direful blow is given   5
Shall light him to behold this trembling murderess,
Pale with my wrongs and ghastly with revenge,
I'll fright his guilty soul to late repentance,
And force him, dying, to confess my justice;
Then, sickly light, shroud thy faint beams forever;   10
Let darkness and oblivion wrap me round:
Though much I fear my blood will prove too vile
To wash the stain of my polluted hands,
Pure or impure, the purple tide shall flow.
How ill this dagger suits my coward mind,   15
And whither would my impetuous rage direct it?
To my Antonio's heart. Oh! Altered love.
Why name I love—is he not basely false?
Will not the babe that trembles in my womb
Bear all its mother's shame, and curse its birth,   20
But that in pity I'll prevent its being,
And save its little head from pointed woe?
Antonio dies, and I pursue his shade
And justify the stroke to worlds above.

Scene iv: The 1705 edition never indicates scene breaks; IV.iii and IV.iv are run together with a single stage direction: "Leads him in and re-enters with a Light and Dagger."
4. Had: Would have
9. justice: justness
10. sickly light: (her own) life
21. But that: Except that
23. pursue his shade: follow his ghost
24. the stroke: (of the knife)

Yet stay, a moment longer let me pause; 25
It cannot be; 'tis madness to imagine;
Can I consent to murder my own soul?
For such Antonio was. Oh! Fatal sound.
He was, but is no more; to me he's lost,
Married again, another claims his truth. 30
Now swift confusion on the adulterous villain,
The rage of injured women fire my breast,
And all the strength of perjured man assist me.
He dies!

Enter ANTONIO [*disguised*]

ANTONIO
What do I see! Impossible. 35
My beauteous love prepared for midnight murder.
Is it the king? Look up, my Margaretta,
Thy husband's come to guard thee.

MARGARETTA
Oh!

She drops the dagger

ANTONIO
What ails my love? My ever gentle goddess, 40
Why art thou thus?

MARGARETTA
From whence art thou?
And by what magic art standest thou before me
To wound my wretched eyes?

ANTONIO
Oh! Answer me. 45

30. truth: loyalty
31. confusion: destruction

Why wert thou armed like a destroying thus,
And why that tragic sound pronounced, he dies?
Who is thy enemy?

MARGARETTA
Oh needless question!
One whom of all mankind I least mistrusted, 50
One who has whispered through these credulous ears
Words so soft they trembled in the utterance,
One whose looks would charm the nicest virgins,
Kindle soft wishes in a vestal's soul,
And fire the heart wrapped round with chilling ice. 55
But he is false, perfidious, and forsworn,
And I resolved to kill him.

ANTONIO
What means my fair?
Hast thou a friend so dear and I not know him?
It cannot be. 60

MARGARETTA
Poor evader,
Look and observe me well, then curse thyself.
To what a fatal precipice of woe,
To what a dismal prospect of despair,
Hast thou and thy ungenerous dealings brought me. 65
My nature, meek and innocent as doves,
Worked up by wrongs was hurrying on to murder.
Oh how the terrible reflection shocks me!
No, I'll no more attempt a crime so horrid,
But live, Antonio, live and boast thy perjuries, 70
But bear thee far away from my upbraidings,
Nor ever meet my injured eyes again.
Farewell, deceiver. (*Going*)

46. like a destroying thus: probably "thus like a destroyer"
51. credulous: trusting
54. vestal: virgin
68. reflection: memory

ANTONIO
Stay, I conjure you stay,
By all those marriage joys we have possessed, 75
By my unaltered truth, my deathless flame,
Oh, stay and solve this most unwelcome riddle.
Resolve me why thou greetest me in this manner
When stealing from the enraged, tumultuous camp
In search of thee, where peace and sweet delight 80
Were used to fix their gentle habitation;
But thou art altered quite, unkind and cruel,
To meet me after all my painful toils
With horror and despair.

MARGARETTA
Have I not cause? 85

ANTONIO
By heaven, no, thou hast no cause to chide.
If to be made the idol of my thoughts,
The constant object of my longing wishes,
The tender business of my doting life,
If these be cause of hate, then I am guilty. 90

MARGARETTA
Yet poorly you could quit me for another.

ANTONIO
Quit thee! Not the world's extended empire
Should bribe me once to think of any other.

MARGARETTA
Have you not married Delia? Quickly fly;
That name again will wake my drowsy rage! 95

---

77. solve: explain
78. Resolve me: Tell me
81. Were used to fix: Used to keep
86. chide: rebuke

ANTONIO
What villain has traduced my honor?
By all that's good, by thy bright self I swear,
I never saw the lady, so innocent
I've not the bare idea of her form.

MARGARETTA
Can this be truth? Or is it possible   100
That honest look should e'er disguise a falsehood?
Did not you come this night like an adulterer,
And was not I as a mistress to receive you,
Denying to the world our marriage rites?
But I, too conscious of pursuing shame,   105
Resolved thy death, nor meant I to survive
But to have told the story and have followed.

ANTONIO
Unthought-of treachery! Oh Margaretta!
Couldst thou so easily believe me guilty?
It was not well, my love!   110

MARGARETTA
Oh, Antonio!
Were I now convinced that thou wert true,
My arms would rivet thee to my beating heart,
And I should die with the excess of joy;
But tell me quickly why thou didst return.   115
Did I not lead thee into yon apartment,
Where I designed
What would have sunk me to the lowest hell?
But tell me, did I not some moments since
Conduct thee thither?   120

ANTONIO
No, by eternal truth.
I with much hazard just this minute found thee

96. traduced: slandered
113. rivet: bind, lock

And came to bear thee from war's raging tumult
To friendly refuge where thou mightst be safe.

MARGARETTA
What can this mean? Or what shall I believe? 125
I only will believe in my Antonio;
I'll trust his charming words and banish fear.
Oh let me hold thee!

ANTONIO
My wife, my dearest blessing,
Who is it has imposed upon thy love? 130
Some lurking villain, some designing traitor,
Whom my sword shall find. (*Going*)

Enter ALVAREZ

ALVAREZ
I have o'erheard
And come prepared to meet your threatening justice.

BOTH:
Alvarez! 135

ALVAREZ
Yes, Alvarez, who loved thee, fair one,
And, being defeated, will not die alone.
        [*Shouting*]
What! Ho, guards here! Treason, murder, treason!

Enter GUARDS, CLOTHARIO *pushing them forward,*
        JAQUEZ *following at a distance*

CLOTHARIO
Make way, that I may follow.

---

23. tumult: confusion

ALVAREZ
My lord Clothario, such discoveries,   140
Such plots against your royal master's life,
My heart bleeds at the hated repetition;
This is Antonio, nephew to the general,
Disguised, and waiting here to kill the king,
And revenge Jacincta's rape.   145

MARGARETTA
Ye sacred powers!
Is poor Jacincta ruined? Who then will wonder
To know we fell a guiltless prey to villainy.

ANTONIO [*to* ALVAREZ]
Vile wretch, what hast thou meant by all these forgeries?
Why do I ask? The meaning is too plain,   150
Inimitable slave.

CLOTHARIO
Speak, Alvarez,
Concerning these assassins, these bold traitors.

ALVAREZ [*pointing*]
See there, my lord, the murderous dagger lies,
Which, had not my auspicious care prevented,   155
Ere this had reeked with royal blood.

CLOTHARIO
Cursed treason!
Seize and to deepest dungeons bear them both;
With eating fetters bind their supple limbs,
And load them to the earth.   160

---

149. forgeries: lies
151. Inimitable slave: Unique villain
156. Ere this: By now
160. load them: weigh them down

ANTONIO

Yet hear me speak,
For death and desolation are abroad;
The tardy vengeance is at last awake,
And tyranny must fall; pursue thy madness,
And blindly bind the hands that should preserve thee,   165
Yet be a man, and spare that innocence.
Fright not her tender nature with rude chains;
See, that arch fiend looks with relenting eyes
And, but for shame, would ask her liberty.
Hast thou no mercy?   170

MARGARETTA

Bind me, bind me quick.
Antonio's only mine, and I am blessed.
On dreadful racks extend my shaking limbs,
My soul shall be unmoved now he is true.
To darkest dungeons bear me, see, I'm ready;   175
Upon the floor I'll kneel, and on my bosom
With softest words I'll lull his piercing sorrows.
Oh! 'Tis impossible to be unhappy,
Thus to die together.

ALVAREZ

Together! What, the traitor and the traitoress?   180
Part them, I charge you; it concerns your safety.
Whilst they are plotting, Rhoderique is in danger.

CLOTHARIO

And with him all his friends.
To several dungeons force them.

162. abroad: outside
166. that innocence: Margaretta
168. that arch fiend: Alvarez
169. ask: ask for
174. now: now (that I know) that
179. Thus: originally, "Thus thus"
183-184. And with him...force them: originally, "and with him all his friends, to / several dungeons force them"

ALVAREZ
Distant as possible. 185

ANTONIO
Most abject villain,
But wait thy just reward; thou canst not miss it.
I scorn to waste another breath upon thee.
    [*to* MARGARETTA]
My ever charming love, submit to hate,
And bear these sufferings with heroic mind; 190
Be sure there is a providence can save us;
Then hope the best, and know I live in thee.

MARGARETTA
Be thou but comforted, and I am calm.
Such joy dwells in thy constant innocence
That grief can find no entrance to my heart. 195
The world shall own the almighty power of love
That can exert a woman to sustain
What boasting stoics would have sunk beneath.
Another tender look, and then farewell.

ANTONIO
Ye juster powers, protect my lovely wife, 200
Soften her jailers with humanity,
And heap on me a double share of woe.
For thy dear sake I can endure, farewell.

CLOTHARIO
Keep a strict guard. The king shall know this matter.

Exeunt ANTONIO *and* MARGARETTA,
led by GUARDS *and* CLOTHARIO

JAQUEZ
In what a gulf of black unfathomed ruin 205

196. own: know, see, acknowledge
198. What: That which

Has my lord plunged himself.

ALVAREZ
Unthinking Jaquez,
On this, thou fearest, I build my happiness,
Since my desired end is Margaretta,
Obtaining her, I am completely happy;   210
With ease I may prevail on dull Clothario
To quit his charge and let me be her keeper;
This feigned discovery has fixed him mine;
Then with unbounded power I'll grasp my prey,
Enjoy and satiate every eager wish,   215
And in one act taste the united pleasure
Of love and towering pride. By heaven I'm pleased
To get the better of contending virtue,
And by my well-contrived successful arts
Blast all the dazzling glories of Antonio.   220

JAQUEZ
Whilst love is all your care, fate has been busy.
Slaughter this night has fed her hungry jaws
And quenched her thirst with streams of Spanish blood.
The Africk captives have revenged their bonds
And sacrificed a life to every ghost   225
That fell this morning from their lighter seat;
With hostile feet they trample round the court
And only pass by this remotest corner.
     (*A shout* [*within*])
Ha, that shout directs the way.

ALVAREZ
Scanty, niggard fortune,   230
Why am I circled in so small a point?
Why thus confined to such a narrow space?

218. contending: resisting
230. niggard: stingy
231. circled...point: surrounded (literally, or by hardships)

This hour must be mine, or all's unrevelled.
       (*More shouts*)
Ha, again, 'tis time to fly the storm.
In this confusion, I may well believe   235
They small distinction make 'twixt friend and foe,
And I'm not yet at leisure to be killed.

Exeunt

---

233. unrevelled: either "unenjoyed" or "unravelled"

Act IV, Scene v

Enter THEOMANTIUS, MULLYMUMEN, and OFFICERS

THEOMANTIUS
Courageous Moor, thy sword has fought with edge, 1
Now justice and revenge both lead thee on.
Twice at the impious head of Rhoderique
I raised the shining steel, and twice drew back,
Conscious it was my king, I durst not strike, 5
But left him to his fate and fought the herd,
Making wild havoc midst his guilty tanders.
Say, my ally, is the loathed tyrant fallen,
And is the noble Julianus safe?
For much incensed he fled from my entreaties 10
And smote the guards I sent to follow him.
Say, does he live?

MULLYMUMEN
[The] king myself took prisoner,
Which, when the stormy Julianus saw,
He cursed his fruitless rage, the turns of chance, 15
And fondly begged to share his master's bonds.
I soon complied.
'Twill teach him to repent his thoughtless virtue
And give us time to slay.

THEOMANTIUS
Forbid, you powers, 20
That awful man, that hoary piety,
Should know one hour's bondage, though he sought it.
Send, quickly send, and beg him to be free.
I'd fly to his release, but well I know
His aged cheeks would glow with angry blushes 25
To be beheld a prisoner.

---

7. tanders: unknown meaning; perhaps "banders," or those who band together

MULLYMUMEN
You are to blame.
'Tis for the common safety most convenient.

THEOMANTIUS
Urge me not, warrior;
I'm not used to dispute where I command, 30
Nor shall I now.

MULLYMUMEN
Small power you boast o'er me.

THEOMANTIUS
Be wise, and cancel not the good thou hast done.
Do not destroy the gratitude I mean thee.
Thou hast been brave, and I'll reward thy valor; 35
Thou to thy native Africk shall return
With half the wealth of ever plenteous Spain;
Each soldier shall have worthy satisfaction.

MULLYMUMEN
Ha, was my sword employed like a base hireling,
Used in necessity and then discharged? 40
I tell thee, prince, not half the wealth you speak of,
Nor half the kingdom shall suffice my ambition.
Know, though too late, I fought not on thy side,
For what had I to do with Spanish broils
But as they served the ends for which I came, 45
Which now I've gained?

THEOMANTIUS
Be warned, nor tempt thy fate;
Though my revenge has led me far, yet know,
Thou shalt not boast one inch of Spanish ground
But what thou dearly buy with Africk blood. 50

---

27. to blame: wrong
39. base hireling: low employee
50. buy: originally, "buy at"

MULLYMUMEN
Forbear thy idle vaunts, mistaken prince;
I now have learned your subtle art of war
And neither want thy aid nor fear thy arms.
Spain shall be all my own.

THEOMANTIUS
Ungrateful Moor, 55
Canst thou so soon forget thou wert my prisoner?

MULLYMUMEN
No, I remember, and I hate thee for it.
But for that chance, I might have been thy friend;
Now I profess myself thy deadliest foe,
And when you trusted me, your fate was angry 60
And doomed you to destruction.

THEOMANTIUS
Yet I am calm.

MULLYMUMEN
Because thou darest not rage;
'Twere bootless to contend with strength like mine.
Vain prince, you meant me for a tool of war, 65
Shortsighted in the depth of politicians:
As such I have used thee, nor canst thou blame me.
Spain and Jacincta now shall be my care.

THEOMANTIUS
Ha, my Jacincta, what will fate do with me?
Monster, thou canst not mean so black a thought. 70
Think'st thou, perfidious fiend, hell's gloomy agent,
Spain has forgot to fight, or Moors to fly,
That thus thou darest betray thy horrid purpose?
But vengeance waits thee.

---

51. vaunts: boasts
64. bootless: pointless

MULLYMUMEN
Swell on, proud enemy, 75
And raise thy boiling indignation high,
To urge thee to the last extremes of passion.
I am thy rival, by thy sullen stars
Chose out to finish thy unhappy fate.
I saw the ravished fair when seeking thee; 80
She fearless ranged the bloody maze of horror,
Calling in vain on cruel Theomantius;
The moon shone fierce to gaze upon her beauties
And lent her willing light to aid my view.
New kindling fires glowed within my breast. 85
I snatched her from the dangers of the night
And sent her to her father, well resolved,
When next we meet, to claim her as my due,
For such she is.

THEOMANTIUS
Cease, profaner, cease, 90
Nor name Jacincta any more, I charge thee.
Base as thou art, restrain thy unhallowed tongue,
Nor with polluted breath sully her whiteness,
But draw, and meet my anger as thou oughtest;
My love and honor both require thy life, 95
And one of us must fall; 'tis so decreed.
Ungrateful, treacherous, barbarian prince,
Thus to reward who gave thee liberty
And ill-used power.

MULLYMUMEN
I laugh at thy vain fury, 100
Nor canst thou fright me from Jacincta's arms.
I love and will possess.

78. stars: fate
80. the ravished fair: Jacincta
81. ranged: traversed
84. her: the moon's
98. who: he who

THEOMANTIUS
By heaven, 'tis false.
Empty as air and vain as children's dreams
Are thy ambitious hopes, thou talking coward. 105

MULLYMUMEN
Coward!

THEOMANTIUS
What less? Thou seest my ready sword,
Yet thine is sheathed.

MULLYMUMEN
I will not please thy vanity,
Nor set vast kingdoms like a common stake 110
To be determined by a single combat,
But to the field again I brave thee, prince.
Thus let thy soldiers try another battle
And, if they dare, make good thy haughty threats.
I shall expect thee. 115

THEOMANTIUS
Villain doubly stamped.
Yes, fear not, I will meet thee to thy cost.
Spain's drooping genius shall again arise
And aid the noble justice of my cause.
Soon as my faithful legions shall hear this, 120
They'll blast thy thoughts of empire and of love,
Defeat thy cursed ambition, give thee up,
A sacrifice to glut my fierce revenge.
Oh, my Jacincta, I refused to see thee
Before I had revenged thy injuries. 125
I fear I have been to blame, but I am coming
To obtain my pardon, or at thy feet expire.

---

110. stake: bet
112. brave: dare, challenge
117. cost: detriment
118. genius: protector

Where is Antonio? I have missed him long.
He fought not by my side as I expected,
Where the good old governor expired.   130
Oh, impious war! Oh fatal, ill-timed treason!
I am involved, and now must wade through all.
Moor, I defy thee; if the powers are just,
They'll throw thee back to what thou meritest most:
Dungeons and chains: rewards for treachery.   135

MULLYMUMEN
Poor, shallow Christian, thoughtless of thy danger.
I tell thee, youth, there lurks around thy shore
Innumerable Africans waiting my summons,
Which, had I fallen, they never heard
But safe returned to their warm native soil.   140
Now a winged messenger brings them swift as wind
To overrun and to possess thy country.

THEOMANTIUS
Dauntless I will oppose thy boasted numbers;
Who fears not grisly death can fear no odds.

MULLYMUMEN
Then let us draw our squadrons up with speed   145
And try again the doubtful chance of battle,
That thou mayst meet me with the highest rage;
Remember bright Jacincta is the conqueror;
Let that alarm thee.

THEOMANTIUS
Oh! Doubt it not, away,   150
And know that heaven and hell as soon may join
As such an angel with a fiend like thee.

130. the good old governor: Don Gomez
139. they never: they never would have
144. Who: He who
148. the conqueror: either "the real winner" or "the conqueror's (prize)"
152. such an angel: Jacincta

Thus traitors learn their folly, though too late,
And, in their sovereign's fall, meet their own fate.

Exeunt

End of Act IV

---

153. traitors: (such as himself)

Act V, Scene i

Scene: a prison. A dim lamp burning

MARGARETTA *comes forward*

MARGARETTA
When shall I wake from this long dream of misery
And shake off all these horrors from my soul:
Rape, murder, treason, wait and watch around,
Each ready to complete my lingering woes.
These prison walls are melancholy scenes
For eyes so young and so unused to sorrows.
Dwells there no genius in this dark abode
Can whisper to my tender, longing heart
Whether my dearest lord be yet alive?
Is there no power, befriending virtuous love,
Will waft my gentle sighs to his soft bosom,
Breathe in his ears my constant vows and prayers,
And arm his faithful breast with distant hope?
Ha! What unexpected lights are these
That with a dismal glare offend my eyes,
Adding new terrors to this place of death?

Enter ALVAREZ *disguised,*
followed by SLAVES *with torches*

ALVAREZ
Spain is no more, her glory's set forever,
Her lofty towers bend their mourning heads
And deep within the center hide their ruins;
Her weeping mothers, and her praying matrons,
Her trembling virgins, all become the prey
Of the insulting, cruel, cursed barbarians.

---

7. genius: helpful spirit
11. Will: That will
20. matrons: old women

Fly, Margaretta, ere these black sons of rapine
Rifle thy sacred beauties.

MARGARETTA
Who art thou, 25
More dreadful to my soul than those thou speakest of,
Where is my lord, canst thou tell aught of him?
If he is lost, I choose to perish here.
Why should I further drag my load of sorrow?

ALVAREZ
Oh, do not trifle precious time in talk! 30
Your faithful lord, impatient of your stay,
Waits for you at a port yet left unseized,
But every moment threatens swift prevention;
Haste, Margaretta, as you love Antonio;
Give me your hand, heaven favor our escape. 35

MARGARETTA
Ha! By the lighted torches' timely light,
And by the fatal voice, it is Alvarez!
Unhand me, hated villain, here I'm fixed,
Here rooted, firm as thy persisting treachery;
Approach me not, ye slaves, he dies that comes. 40

ALVAREZ
Death, how they stand
As if they were thunderstruck with empty words.
Come near, ye coward slaves, and bear her hence.

They struggle. MARGARETTA *gets
loose and draws a dagger.*

---

23. rapine: seizure, rape
24. Rifle: Seize
30. trifle: waste
41. Death: an oath

MARGARETTA
Stand off, base wretch; see, I am armed for violence:
This useful steel in the palace I secured, 45
Lest I again might meet a fiend like thee.

ALVAREZ
Ill-fated villainy!

MARGARETTA
If thou comest on, that very moment, know,
Or in thy cursed bosom or my own,
By all that's chaste, I'll plunge this ready dagger, 50
Though in the deed I do a double murder
And kill an unborn innocent.

ALVAREZ
Let me think.

MARGARETTA
Do, if thou canst, think, and abhor thy guilt.
Twice hast thou urged my unstained hands to murder, 55
To break all laws, both human and divine;
And canst thou yet resolve to send my soul
I know not whither to escape pollution?
Where then, alas, will be your fruitless wishes
When ghastly death shall have defaced my form? 60
Then all your raging fires will soon extinguish.

ALVAREZ
Your words and your undaunted mind have conquered,
Struck on my hardened sense, and waked reflection.
    (*Kneeling*)
Be gone all thoughts of love and brutal force.
Here in deep penitence let me ever kneel 65
To heaven and this offended fair for pardon.

---

49. Or: Either
52. an unborn innocent: her child

But oh! It is too much, too much to hope;
Inspire her then, ye angry juster powers,
To strike my guilty breast, but guard her bosom,
Softer and whiter than the falling snow, 70
Pure as unspotted crystal, chaste as the emerald.
>   *During this speech, he creeps insensibly nearer and*
>   *nearer, till starting of a sudden he seizes her hand*
>   *and wrests the dagger.*

Now you are mine again!

MARGARETTA
Deceitful fiend!
Stay, oh, stay!

ALVAREZ
Not one doubtful moment; 75
Thus will I bear my lovely destined prize
Through towering flames or thousand clashing swords
And pass undaunted to the goal of love.

MARGARETTA
Help, help, ye powers, some help!

Enter ANTONIO *and* SOLDIERS

ANTONIO
It is my love! 80
What impious slave has thus increased her terrors?
>   [*Stabs* ALVAREZ]

I think my sword has reached thee.

ALVAREZ
'Twas well directed.
>   (*Falls*)

ANTONIO
My dearest wife.

78. undaunted: unimpeded

MARGARETTA
My blessed deliverer. 85

ANTONIO
Say who again pursued thy innocence.

ALVAREZ
A worthless wretch, that fain would die unknown,
But 'twill not be.

ANTONIO
I know thee well, thou villain,
And know thee for the most unheard-of wretch, 90
The basest, and the ripest for destruction,
And 'twas most just in fate my sword should end thee.

ALVAREZ
It was. The raging blood flows out apace,
And now I see my shame, and loathe myself.
My eyes grow dim in the thick shade of death, 95
And horrid visions press my ebbing soul;
A thousand ghastly phantoms fleet before me,
Fruitless remorse, confusion and despair,
With all their knotted scorpions lash my conscience.
Would I had died in battle! Oh, forgive me. 100

MARGARETTA
I do, for now thou dost repent in earnest.

ALVAREZ
Oh, take thy dazzling beauties from my view!
Life, though in anguish, lingers to behold thee,
But turn thy lovely face, and I expire.

Dies

87. fain: gladly
93. raging: lustful
93. apace: quickly

ANTONIO
He's gone, and what I could not once have thought: 105
The man I've called my friend and long-esteemed
Companion of my youth and of my fame,
Now weltering in his blood, slain by my hand.
He merits not one tear.

MARGARETTA
His faults die with him. 110
But tell me, my Antonio, how camest thou
Like some blessed spirit to my timely aid
When hope was lost?

ANTONIO
Set free by Theomantius,
With careful haste I sought the palace round, 115
Nor left a slave unasked till I had found thee;
Swift as the wind, I flew to break thy chains,
And oh, ye powers, I gave thee double liberty.
But to what refuge shall I bear thee now?
The Moors, alas, surround us every way, 120
And this is near the prison of the king
Where most there rage will aim. Instruct me, heaven,
If innocence and virtue be your care,
Oh, hear a lover's and a husband's prayer!
Preserve my wife, and save me from despair. 125

Exeunt

---

115. the palace round: all around the palace
118. double liberty: from prison and from Alvarez

Act V, Scene ii

*Scene draws and discovers an inner prison,
from whence the KING comes forward*

KING
Down, ye tormenting thoughts, where would ye drive me?
I stand already on the verge of madness;
Oh, altered state, no sign of former majesty!
The fawning throng that worshiped at my feet
And watched the earliest motion of my eyes   5
Are now no more; jailers supply their places,
With sternest looks and rough, ill-mannered words;
Instead of flatterers, my crimes attend me,
And gall my memory with hated truths;
Hence, ye unwelcome, numerous intruders,   10
Saucy companions of my solitude.
In vain I banish what will still return
With added strength, rebounding to my torture.
Lust, rapine, secret fraud and open violence:
Ingratitude, thou every vice in one,   15
In all your hideous forms I view ye now,
And Julianus and Jacincta's wrongs
Are ever present to my haunted fancy.

Enter JULIANUS behind him

JULIANUS
Who is it, in these caves that lead to death,
Breaks the deep silence with those wretched names? 20
Speak what thou art, who kindly dost lament
Poor Julianus and Jacincta's fate?

KING
The general's voice. Fall, fall, ye massy pillars

---

10. Hence: Away
11. saucy: rude

That bear this house of sorrow, fall and crush me;
Ascend, ye sickly vapors from below, 25
And quickly blast me with your baneful damps,
Convulsive pangs, life's painful, latest struggle,
When, like the drops on these unwholesome walls,
Cold, clammy dews shall bathe my dying limbs,
Nor death, nor fear of punishments behind 30
Can shock my soul like Julianus' sight.

JULIANUS
If grief has not too far confused my sense,
Those mournful sounds confess the unhappy king;
I've listened to that voice in happier hours,
And if I guess I aright, it is the king. 35

KING (*aside*)
It was the king, and still I am myself.
Now let me summon all my innate greatness
That I may meet this faulty, injured man
And boldly face him with a mind resolved.
    [*to* JULIANUS]
See, Julianus, and indulge thy hate; 40
Glut thy pleased sight with fallen Rhoderique,
And when thou hast gazed enough, exalt thy arm,
And print in bloody characters thy vengeance.
I am prepared for fate.

JULIANUS
Mistaken king! 45
It is not in thy hoodwinked destiny
To judge aright of suffering Julianus.
Forsaken and a prisoner like you,
I have no sword to punish thy injustice,

---

25. sickly vapors from below: diseased air, from under the ground or from hell
33. confess: give away
42. exalt thy arm: (with murder/vengeance)
47. aright: accurately

Or, if I had, I durst be loyal still. 50
Yet I will wound thy ears with such sad words
That if thy nature be not wholly savage
Shall strike thee deeper than the sharpest steel.

KING
Thus subtle traitors ever watch their time,
Like the ungenerous race of coward brutes 55
Who, when the lion's fettered in the toils,
Insult the majesty that just before
They trembled to behold.

JULIANUS
Dost rouse me, king?
Then what I meant an humble soft reproof, 60
Gentle, to wake repentance and no more,
Shall now become an eating corrosive
And gall thy hardened temper to the quick.
Oh fatal Rhoderique! Why stop my words?
So long I've learned and practiced to obey, 65
I cannot force my tongue to a rebellion,
Yet thou hast wronged me, and heaven owns the quarrel.
Spain is this hour sinking by thy vices.
Some baneful planet reigned when thou wert born
And laid up all her sad effects in thee. 70
The hungry famine and the blue-eyed pestilence
Are mercies to the mischiefs of this night:
Mischiefs thy unexampled crimes have wrested
From the supreme avengers.

KING
Peace, thou dotard, 75

56. fettered in the toils: ensnared in a trap
59. rouse: berate
60. meant: meant as
63. gall: chafe
67. owns: acknowledges, approves
68. by: because of
73. unexampled: unrivaled

Nor dare to tax the everlasting justice
As the abettor of thy monstrous treason,
Impious rebel.

JULIANUS [*aside*]
Indignation chokes me,
Yet I'll surmount it. Be thyself, old man,   80
Nor let ungoverned rage o'ercome thy virtue.
       [*to* KING]
Ungrateful tyrant, sure it can be no fault
To give thee titles thou so truly meritest;
Tell me why I alone, from all the crowd
Of passive slaves that bowed beneath thy yoke,   85
Was chose to bear the burden of thy shame.
Why was my loyalty so ill rewarded,
The ancient honor of my house profaned,
My age pursued with most unheard-of wrongs,
Pressed to the grave with hoary infamy?   90
Why used thus hardly?

KING
Are subjects to contend with royal power?
What was thy house, or all thy boasted race,
To be esteemed in balance with my pleasures?
Hadst thou been loyal, as thou wouldst insinuate,   95
Thou hadst not grudged a daughter to thy king:
That petty sacrifice thousands would offer,
But thou, blinded with pride and vanity,
Thinkest it more noble to undo thy country
Than to endure the smallest injury   100
Mean and unworthy.

JULIANUS
Falsely thou dost upbraid me.

---

76. tax the everlasting justice: accuse heaven
83. titles: e.g. "tyrant"
94. in balance: in comparison
96. grudged: begrudged
101. Mean: Low

Had I been father to a hundred children,
All innocent and bright as my Jacincta,
And hadst thou torn them all from my fond care   105
And given them up to ignominious slavery,
Or if to indulge a cruel thirst of blood
Thou hadst doomed them to be slain before my face,
I had lamented but ne'er sought revenge.

KING
Then why does thy old age put on this mask   110
Of insolent, unnecessary anger?
Why roll thy gloomy eyes with such strong fury,
Why swell thy empty veins, why shake thy limbs,
For such a trifling wrong?

JULIANUS
Oh! Rhoderique, thou hast undone my fame,   115
Buried my glory in a living tomb,
Entailed eternal shame upon my memory;
My poor child, blotted by thy monstrous lust,
Wanders about, a restless misery,
A weeping anguish.   120

KING
I'll hear no more.

JULIANUS
Yes, thou shalt hear me, king,
Till I have changed this prison to a hell
And forced thee to anticipate the woes
Prepared for sinking tyrants.   125

KING
Fury and torture!
Is there no way to free me from this slave,

---

106. ignominious: disgraceful
109. had: would have
125. Prepared: (by heaven and hell)

This loud reviler of his fallen monarch?
Have not I left one open path to death?
Are all the numerous adamantine gates 130
By wayward fate made fast against the wretched?

JULIANUS
Ha! What have I done? I fear I've gone too far.
Forgive me, sir, sorrow has turned my brain.
See, at your feet I throw the rash offender.
   [*throws himself down*]
Though you have erred, yet still you are my king, 135
Not less in this dark solitary prison
Than when you filled the awful throne of Spain.
Oh! If there yet remained one glance of pity
In gentle mercy's unexhausted store,
Forgetting all my wrongs, my loads of griefs, 140
These aged knees would grow one piece with earth
To implore it for your safety.

KING
I'd despise it.
Both life and empire are below my care.
Who can resolve me what's beyond this span? 145
Perhaps I may return to my first nothing.
Oh! What a happy state were long oblivion,
Forgetting and forgot, relieved from thought,
From torturing memory and vain remorse:
'Twere lasting peace, uninterrupted rest, 150
A sweet, sound sleep to all eternity:
This were worth asking.

JULIANUS
Forbear these mournful thoughts.

---

128. reviler: insulter
130. Adamantine: unbreakable
131. made fast: sealed tight
145. resolve: teach
145. this span: life

Ye impartial beings, was it your decree
That I, who loved my country and my king 155
Dearer than life,
That I should be the unassisting cause
Of all the black confusion of this night?
From my unhappy loins the guiltless maid
Sprung to fulfill the irrevocable doom. 160
Oh! Wounding grief, incessant lamentation,
Not to be borne.

KING
Can he feel pangs like these?
He that has done no wrong, is just and pious?
Then what must be my lot, oh Julianus! 165
Though I have long been cursed with purple greatness,
I never, never knew an hour like this.
Flattered in vice, I had no time to reflect.
Alas! Why was I brought within thy reach
To feel the sacred influence of thy virtue 170
And mourn my crimes, when there's no hope of pardon?

JULIANUS
Do not despair.
When most severe I seemed, yet even then,
Spite of my injuries, you were my care.
Upon my surly jailers I've prevailed 175
To find my daughter and to bring her here.
She yet has power o'er Theomantius' soul.

KING
Enough, enough,
Press me not more with overwhelming shame.
In vain I struggle in this crowd of thoughts 180
To express my sense of thy amazing goodness;
The faltering accents hang upon my tongue,
And now I'd kneel to thee wouldst thou permit it.

166. purple: royal
174. Spite: In spite

THE CONQUEST OF SPAIN

JULIANUS
No more of this. Oh, king! My heart bleeds for thee.
Why was thy noble nature led astray?   195
Why didst thou take base villains to thy bosom
And banish all thy aged counselors
That would have reined thy looser appetites
And gently led thee in the paths of virtue?
I fear 'tis now too late.   200

KING
'Tis just it should,
Since 'tis not in my power to heal the sorrows
I have heaped upon thy lovely, rifled daughter,
That fairest piece that ever nature drew,
Stained and defaced by my cursed violence.   205
Oh, is it fit so vile a wretch should live?
No. As I have done the wrongs I can't repair,
Inevitable vengeance wails to sink me,
Yet ere I fall, oh thou superior man,
Forgive a royal suppliant.   210

JULIANUS
So at my latest moment
May gracious heaven extend the arms of mercy
And pardon all the errors of my life
As I forgive the injuries thou hast done me.
These withered hands shall still be lifted up   215
To beg thou may'st escape, if possible,
The threatened danger.

KING
Such wrongs as thine, so generously forgiven,
Will never be believed in aftertimes.
Oh, had I power!   220
A mighty reparation I would offer.

198. reined: reined in, controlled
203. rifled: robbed
221. A mighty reparation: that is, an offer to marry Jacincta

But 'tis in vain to talk: I have no crown,
Or, if I had, Jacincta would have scorned it.
Another had her vows.

JULIANUS
Ill-fated vows. 225
My king, my darling daughter, and my country,
Each of you miserable in extreme,
While Julianus suffers in you all.
But hark! My child. That signal says she's here.
Once more my aching eyes shall view her sweetness 230
And pay a mournful tribute to her fate.

KING
Oh, let me fly.
In the lowest cell of darkness I would hide me
Among pale specters of despair and horror,
So I may shun that lovely ruined fair 235
Whose violated form I dare not meet.
Oh, Julianus! Oh, Jacincta!

Exit

JULIANUS
'Tis easy to resign the dregs of life.
My sand runs low in the dull course of age.
Should fate not shake the glass, 'twould soon be out. 240

Enter JACINCTA, *wounded*

JACINCTA
Pensive he stands. When will my woes be full?

JULIANUS
Come near, thou child of sorrow,

224. Another: Someone else
239. My sand: as in an hourglass
240. shake the glass: change course (literally, interfere with the hourglass)
241. full: finished

Thou wretched offspring of a poor old man
That has outlived that mighty hoard of fame
His active youth laid up in a full harvest. 245
Ha, what means that blood upon thy snowy breast?
Thou art not wounded?

JACINCTA
Oh, 'twas a friendly sword.
A band of Moors were guarding me to you
At the command of their imperious general 250
When some of your poor, faithful soldiers knew me
And, fearing they had seized me as a prey,
Soon forced them to resign their trembling charge.
In the rude scuffle, some relenting power
Leveled this wound in pity to my sufferings. 255
Now be at peace and smile again, my father.
I was the fatal period of your honor,
And from my ashes, like another phoenix,
Glory once more shall rise.

JULIANUS
I know it well, 260
Glory will rise and shine upon our tombs,
For I shall soon o'ertake thy gentle shade.
Among the few that served unbiased virtue,
Sure we may find an honorable grave.
Why dost thou weep, where are the roses now 265
That dwelt in lively colors on those cheeks,
Pale as approaching death? Oh, my Jacincta!
I have but one request, and all is finished:
Couldst thou but see rash Theomantius thus,
Thy dying words would charm his headlong rage 270
And move his soul to save the unhappy king
Who now repents his crimes.

251. knew: recognized
257. period: end
262. shade: ghost
270. charm: ease

JACINCTA
I knew your piety
And sent a trusty slave to guide him hither,
But could you feel the tortures of my breast, 275
The shaking agonies, the bleeding love
I sink beneath at thoughts of seeing him,
Indeed you'd pity me.
Great is thy work, and for thy country's good
Exert thyself. Ha, what noise is that? 280

Shouts and noises of clashing swords without

[WITHOUT]
Which way? The king? You die if you resist.

JULIANUS
Seek they the king? Then my fate tears me from thee,
If possible, to save him;
If not, at least I shall meet noble death.
Farewell. 285

JACINCTA
Oh, stay, my father, yet ere we part,
For we shall never, never meet again,
Will you not lay by all that majesty
Which strikes your enemies with awful terror,
And be all love, all tenderness, all parent 290
To an only child, who begs your latest blessing?

JULIANUS
Why wouldst thou triumph o'er thy father's weakness
And force the aged sluice to send up tears,
When thirsty grief has drained the exhausted springs?
Why wouldst thou see me like a boy lament 295

274. him: Theomantius
291. latest: final
293. sluice: dam

A most immense, inevitable loss?
But veil that wound from my tormented eyes.
       (JACINCTA *draws her veil over her bosoms*)
Believe me, child, these drops more hardly flow
Than all those streams of blood I lost in battle.

JACINCTA
Alas, I cannot bear the killing sight.   300
Oh, weep no more.

JULIANUS [*kneeling*]
Thus let me bend to earth.

JACINCTA
Why kneels my father?

JULIANUS
To ask thy pardon that I did beget thee;
From me, the fatal source of misery,   305
Thou drewest thy wretched being.

JACINCTA
Oh, forbear!
'Tis true, you are my dearest, godlike father,
You gave me life in an unhappy hour,
But shame and meager woe lagged far behind,   310
Nor were you parent of my ruin.

JULIANUS
No!
I loved thee with uncommon tenderness,
Even such as none but thee could e'er deserve,
But thou wert all perfection, all obedience.   315
Methinks I see the angels hovering o'er thee,

---

298. drops: tears
298. hardly: painfully
309. unhappy: unlucky

Surrounded with an host of smiling saints,
Who seem to wish and wait for thy reception.
Tell them thou'rt coming to receive their welcomes.
From heaven I had thee, and to heaven again   320
Early thou wilt return, refined by sufferings;
There mayst thou feast on joys which earth denied;
There we again shall meet, to part no more.

JACINCTA
Wafted on the blessed wings of your just prayers,
Methinks I am there already.   325

WITHOUT
Follow, and revenge the injured general.

JULIANUS
Now, by my wrongs, the voice of Spanish rage.
Soon I'll rebuke their guilty, headlong error.
Heaven has decreed I shall not close thy eyes;
That last kind office I leave to Theomantius.   330

WITHOUT
This way, this way.

JULIANUS
I come! Oh, Jacincta!
But let me hold thee to my heart a moment,
Then, with a parting, cold, paternal kiss
Resign thee patiently to death and fate.   335
Oh cruel sounds, my soul fleets after thee,
And my eyes strain their balls to the dear object.
It must not be, oh nature, heart, Jacincta.

[*Exit*]

---

323. to part no more: The 1705 edition directs Julianus exit here.
329. close thy eyes: (in death)
336. fleets after: longs to follow
337. the dear object: unclear meaning; perhaps Jacincta

THE CONQUEST OF SPAIN 129

JACINCTA
Farewell, farewell forever.
He's gone, and a dark gloom begins to shade me. 340
This wound will set the imprisoned soul at liberty,
Though very gently it performs its work,
As loath to part from the rich balm of life.
Oh, death: thou remedy of mind's distress!
Approach, and take me to thy long embrace. 345
Oh, Theomantius! Hark, I hear him coming,
But the poor heart that used to beat his welcome,
Now laboring in the pain of desolation,
Neglects the lover.

Enter THEOMANTIUS

THEOMANTIUS
What dismal, silent, dark abode is this? 350
Sure 'tis the mansion of despairing lovers
Where all that groan beneath oppressing fate,
Like Theomantius and Jacincta cursed,
Sadly repair to vent their swelling griefs.
And thou, my love, like the bright goddess here 355
Display'st a mournful glory all around
And makest even ruin lovely.

JACINCTA
Hold yet, my spirits;
Let me collect a little, little force,
A moment's life, and I have done forever. 360
Oh, Theomantius, how is fortune changed
Since t'other day's gaudy, deluding prospect.
Our early loves seemed the blessed care of heaven
And promised all that hopeful youth could wish,
Serene and clear as ever-gentle peace, 365

343. As loath: As if reluctant
348. desolation: probably "dissolution," or death; conversely, "desolation"
354. repair: return, retire

No darkening cloud threatened our halcyon state,
And yet the rowling tempest lay behind.
At length it broke: the mighty curse came down
And dashed our meeting joys.

THEOMANTIUS
Oh, gnawing truth! 370

JACINCTA
Much Rhoderique has to answer for his crimes,
But thou art guiltier far.

THEOMANTIUS
Heartbreaking words!
Why does my cruel fair one treat me thus?
Have I not shared her injuries and griefs, 375
And paid a stream of blood for every tear
That tyranny has forced from her loved eyes?
And could I give her pain?

JACINCTA
Witness my ruined country.
But oh! The slaughtered heaps of noble Spaniards, 380
Oh! Could you think this would not give me pain?
Hard is my task, and most severe my fate,
That in this latest scene of yielding life,
When all the kindest, softest, tender things
That faithful lovers know should be expressed 385
Instead of these, alas! My dying words
Must blame my Theomantius.

THEOMANTIUS [*kneeling*]
Soul-rending torture!
Forbear to wound me with your just reproach.
Left stung with deep remorse, I fall before you, 390
A victim to your anger.

366. halcyon: happy, golden

THE CONQUEST OF SPAIN

JACINCTA
Tell me why,
When, putting off my timorous sex's fears,
Between the lifted spears I ran to seek thee,
Why did my cries not stop thy barbarous arm 395
From further slaughter?

THEOMANTIUS
Some unseen power,
Fixed on Spain's destruction, hurried me on,
And those vile injuries thou hadst received
O'erwhelmed that reason which would else have heard 400
And readily obeyed thee.

JACINCTA
Rash revenge!
Now what canst thou expect, unhappy prince,
But the reward that's due to headlong rage:
To wander here on earth, despised and hated, 405
And, when thou diest, to be excluded heaven?
For no presumptuous punishers of kings
Will be admitted to those blessed abodes.
Thither, the loyal and unshaken virtue
Can only wing its flight. 410

THEOMANTIUS
Recall thy piercing words.
Thus crawling on the earth like a vile slave,
Let thy relenting justice bless my penitence.
Already I am punished for my crimes;
The ungrateful Moor turns the sword I gave him 415
To his deliverer's throat and vows my fall.

398. Fixed: Set
400. else: otherwise
409-410. Thither...flight: Only the loyal and virtuous can fly there (to heaven)
412. crawling on the earth: The 1705 edition directs Theomantius to kneel here instead of in his previous speech

But let him triumph, do but thou forgive,
Call my dire fault the effect of truest love,
And I am satisfied.

JACINCTA
Rise, Theomantius.   420
And if thou canst repair thy fatal error—
But much I doubt—
My willing soul shall hold thee dear as ever,
But much I doubt.

THEOMANTIUS (*rising hastily*)
Banish thy fears.   425
Inspired by thee, I shall do miracles.
There is one hope yet left, my lovely fair,
And now you have given me leave to expect a pardon,
My future actions shall deserve your mercy.
The brave Antonio heads a bold reserve   430
Who will sell their lives too dear for Africk purchase;
With them again we'll turn the giddy scale
And save our sinking nation.

JACINCTA
'Tis well, and now I've nothing left to do,
Oh, Theomantius!   435

THEOMANTIUS
Ha! What means my love?
A deadly paleness triumphs in thy face,
And tremblings seize thee.

JACINCTA (*lifts up the veil*)
See this fatal wound:

---

422. But much I doubt: In the 1705 edition, this line is printed as a continuation of the previous line; given the odd placement and the line's repeating at line 424, this first occurrence may have been added in error.
428. now: now that
430. a bold reserve: (of soldiers)
431. dear: expensive

THE CONQUEST OF SPAIN

The welcome present of an unknown arm 440
Who did not mean the kind relief to me.
Thy hand, for I am sinking.

THEOMANTIUS [*taking her hand*]
Sink all nature,
Heap on this burdened wretch the weight of worlds,
They cannot crush like this. Once more speak to me, 445
Thou lovely fading beauty, bless my soul
With one kind syllable e'er thou takest thy wing
To the bright realms above, thy native home.
Speak, though to increase despair and add to my distraction.

JACINCTA
I love thee, and a temper nice as mine 450
In these few tender words sums up the whole.
There's something takes thy pleasing form away;
Where art thou vanished from dazzling eyes?
Darkness comes on, and I can search no further.

Dies

THEOMANTIUS
Who shall I curse, to whom shall I complain? 455
If within this loathsome horrid vault
There has been frequent murders, foulest rapine,
Distorting racks, and penetrating fires,
With all the barbarous cruelties of rage
That hell and fierce revenge could e'er inspire, 460
Yet have their woes been sports compared with mine.
    (*He draws*)
Still here's a friend that will afford me comfort
And guide the dusky way to endless peace.
Antonio, lead the army; I'll rest here.
Look down, Jacincta, view my resolution. 465

450. nice: simple
456. vault: prison

I could not strike more heartily in thy revenge.
    (*Falls on his sword*)

Enter an OFFICER *and* SOLDIERS

OFFICER
Where's Theomantius?

THEOMANTIUS
What wouldst thou?

OFFICER
Spain is no more; this hour dates her fall.
New-landing Moors have covered all the strand,   470
Encompassing the only troops were left,
Led by Antonio, who resists in vain,
For they are taken all, or perished.

THEOMANTIUS
Hateful news.
Help, soldiers, and lay me by that dear one.   475
On thy cold lips I leave my dying sorrows,
    [*Kisses* JACINCTA]
And now, all's well.

Dies

OFFICER
Alas! What noise is that of clashing swords?
The enemy pursues us.

Enter several MOORS, *driving in* JULIANUS, *wounded*

FIRST MOOR
Yield, and be safe.   480

---

471. were: who were

JULIANUS
I scorn the offer.
Let these wounds inform your savage eyes
That Julianus knows not to submit.

OFFICER
Where is the king?

JULIANUS
I hope he is escaped. 485

SECOND MOOR
'Twas by thy aid, for which this shall reward thee.

As they engage, enter MULLYMUMEN, *his sword drawn, several* PRISONERS, CLOTHARIO *and* LODOVICUS *bound, and* OFFICERS. MULLYMUMEN *speaks entering.*

MULLYMUMEN
Here let insatiate death restrain his arm.
Preserve the general; save great Julianus;
Long may he live.

JULIANUS
Who wishes me that curse? 490
But I am past its power. Here end my sufferings.
Ill fate can wound no more.

MULLYMUMEN
Thou only Spaniard,
What impious hand durst pierce thy worthy breast
That held the noblest art of humankind? 495
Oh, say! Who did this most accursed deed?

---

483. knows not: knows not how
493. only: unique
495. art: skill

SECOND MOOR
'Twas I. He has given Rhoderique liberty,
Led him from prison with undaunted courage,
And urged the Spanish soldiers to his side;
Them we soon conquered, but he mocked our fury,   500
And with his naked breast maintained the passage
Whilst the king escaped.

MULLYMUMEN
He must be taken,
But no matter. That at our better leisure.
Here all my rage is turned to fruitless pity.   505
Worthy general, my help.

JULIANUS
Away,
Approach me not with thy unwelcome care.
Hast thou not ruined my loved, native country,
Possessed my unpolluted mother earth?   510
And wouldst thou offer me detested help?
There's a magnetic force bends me this way
Towards these dear bodies of my children.
Moor, if thou wouldst be kind to Julianus,
Lay me in one tomb with these loved relics.   515

MULLYMUMEN
It shall be done.

Enter OFFICERS, *with* ANTONIO
and MARGARETTA *prisoners*

OFFICER
Behold this lovely pair,
Whom we took just making to the port.

---

501. maintained: defended
503. He: The king
504. at our better leisure: in good time

THE CONQUEST OF SPAIN

JULIANUS
My foster children: yet another pang.

MARGARETTA
My dear Jacincta, dead! Oh, my father! 520

ANTONIO
The general dying, Theomantius dead.
Oh fatal hour, cruel, heart-wounding sight.

MULLYMUMEN
Rash Theomantius' fall let lovers mourn,
For only they know to excuse his fault.
O'er that bright form, should I give way to grief, 525
I could myself be prodigal of tears.
But this great man, superior to our praise,
Is such a loss as sorrow can't express;
Here turn your watery eyes, ye captive Spaniards;
He merits endless wailings. 530

JULIANUS
Oh, Mullymumen!
If in thy warlike heart compassion reign,
Then let this mournful pair in peace remove
Far from the sight of desolated Spain
To Antonio's distant province; there secure, 535
They never will molest thy unenvied state.
Jacincta, Theomantius, I am coming;
Take to your shades the wretched Julianus.
My painful, tedious hours at last are finished,

---

519. pang: (of grief)
524. know to: know how to
525. that bright form: Jacincta
526. prodigal: liberal, wasteful
527. this great man: Julianus
533. this mournful pair: Margaretta and Antonio
536. molest: bother
538. your shades: your ghosts, yourselves

And balmy rest steals o'er my wearied lids. 540
No more, but mercy, and I'm with ye.

Dies

MULLYMUMEN
He sleeps forever. Fly, ye beauteous mourners;
The mighty general obtained your freedom.
    [*to* SOLDIERS]
Guard them to the port.
    (*Turning to the other prisoners* [CLOTHARIO *and*
    LODOVICUS])
Bear these to death. 545

ANTONIO
For life and liberty,
Scarce can I bend my soul to thank thee, Moor.
But, for thy dearest sake, my lovely wife,
I'll bear to live and leave these faithful friends,
Which else I wish to follow. 550

MARGARETTA
Oh, heavy parting,
But I will smother my complaints in silence
And, having all in thee, praise the high powers.
Left by vain grief, I pull down new misfortunes.

Exeunt ANTONIO *and* MARGARETTA *with* SOLDIERS

FIRST MOOR
Now, great sir, the nation's wholly yours, 555
And all wait ready to salute you king.

ALL
Long live the prosperous, royal Mullymumen.

---

544. them: Margaretta and Antonio
550. I: I'd

MULLYMUMEN
A tomb magnificent and great to these I'll raise,
And then pursue the flying Rhoderique.
From this auspicious hour we date our reign,   560
The first of Moors that ever conquered Spain.

Exeunt

End of Act V

---

558. these: the dead

MARY PIX

An Epilogue, by a Friend

    You've seen the unhappy monarch's wretched fate   1
Who to the best of subjects proved ingrate:
No wonder he sat loose upon his throne
After such treatment to its supporter shown.
    How happy is our isle, which can't complain   5
That her great hero has deserved in vain!
Gladly we've seen the senate and the crown
Making their gratitude, like his renown,
Forever to succeeding ages known.
    You, fairest charmers, to whose gentle sway   10
With pleasure we submit and choose t'obey,
Whom to offend base cowards only dare,
And those whom nothing else can frighten fear,
He runs a double risk that injures you,
Breaking the allegiance to your beauties due,   15
And must expect our sex his enemies too.
We've seen the greatest powers prove no defense
To him that wronged your unarmed innocence.
The generous warriors scorn to assert his cause
Who's violated honor's sacred laws.   20
    None are so brave as those whom you inspire
With life and vigor from love's active fire:
When you our willing hands and hearts command,
Our daring onsets nothing can withstand.
We fear no darts but from your piercing eyes,   25
And every terror but your frowns despise.

3. loose: insecurely
4. its supporter: Julianus
5. our isle: England (contrasted with Spain)
10. fairest charmers: women
16. our sex: probably men, as the prologue seems to be spoken by a man
19. assert: defend
20. Who's: Who has
24. daring onsets: brave deeds
26. And every...despise: And despise every terror except for your frowns

    Thus when in mighty Anna's cause we fight,
Toils are our pleasures: dangers, our delight.
Since to maintain her rights we've used our arms,
They've proved resistless as her powerful charms 30
Whose influence has in one campaign done more
Than we in ages could perform before.
    Still may your smiles and victories reward;
Their happy progress nothing shall retard.
All the united powers of France and Spain, 35
Our fearless legions shall oppose in vain.
To grace your glorious triumphs, both shall join,
And their lost trophies at your feet resign.

The End

27. Anna: Anne Stuart, queen at this time of this play
30. proved: proved as
33. Still: Ever
34. retard: slow
36. Our fearless legions shall oppose in vain: That is, "Shall oppose our fearless legions in vain"

From the Editor

Thank you for reading *The Conquest of Spain*. I am happy to have been able to share this play with you. If you enjoyed this story and this edition, it will mean a great deal to me and to future readers if you leave a review on the website you purchased it from. Reviews make an immense impact on the reach of a book.

There is a great wealth of untapped literature in the world, but it is not easy for most people to find. It has been a passion project of mine to create this little volume and to get Mary Pix's work into the world in a simple, accessible, and accurate format. I hope I have succeeded in doing that.

If you would like to reach out to me directly with any feedback or regarding any possible improvements, please contact me at **conquestofspain@gmail.com**.

www.ingramcontent.com/pod-product-compliance
Lightning Source LLC
Chambersburg PA
CBHW022017290426
44109CB00015B/1202